a HOUSE DIVIDED

BOOKS IN THE Lifelines for Recovery SERIES

Zondervan's Lifelines for Recovery Series emphasizes
healthy, step-by-step approaches for dealing with spe-
cific critical issues.

a HOUSE DIVIDED

THE SECRET BETRAYAL—INCEST

KATHERINE EDWARDS

PYRANEE
BOOKS

Zondervan Publishing House
Grand Rapids, Michigan

A House Divided
Copyright © 1990 by Katherine Edwards

A Pyranee Book
Published by the Zondervan Publishing House
1415 Lake Drive, S.E., Grand Rapids, Michigan 49506

Library of Congress Cataloging-in-Publication Data

Edwards, Katherine.
    A house divided : the secret betrayal—incest / Katherine
Edwards.
        p. cm.
    Includes bibliographical references.
    ISBN 0-310-43381-9
    1. Edwards, Katherine. 2. Incest victims—United
States—
    Biography. 3. Sexually abused children—United States—
Biography.
    4. Fathers and daughters—United States. I. Title.
    HQ72.U53E383   1990
    362.7'6—dc20   89–70191
                                                              CIP

Unless otherwise noted, all Scripture references are taken
from the *Holy Bible: New International Version* (North
American Edition), copyright © 1973, 1978, 1984 by the
International Bible Society. Used by permission of Zondervan Bible Publishers.

Printed in the United States of America

90 91 92 93 94 95 / AK / 10 9 8 7 6 5 4 3 2 1

This book is for Hadley,
without whom much of what
is good in my life would
never have happened.

CONTENTS

This has been an unusual year, a year of unusual lessons, many of them learned through the pages that follow.

I came to the task of writing this book confident that I could do the job, and found that I could not. On several occasions, after staring blankly at the keyboard of my typewriter for two weeks, with a partially completed manuscript on my hands, I was brought to the end of myself. On my knees, in tears, I was forced to ask the Lord to continue the work through me.

Three times I nearly destroyed the manuscript, but at each temptation to do so I realized that another copy was in the hands of a friend. Destruction would accomplish nothing. By the time all copies were restored to me, my cold feet had warmed.

Other temptations arose, too—some that I had no will to resist: temptations to self-pity and the renewal of old grievances, temptations to strike out at those who had hurt me. I had strength only to ask the Lord to give me the will to obey Him. Unusual, perhaps, but it was an unusual situation, and our God is not limited to ordinary circumstances.

From the perspective of time I have regained my grasp of the "why" of these pages, and my commitment is renewed. Writing this story has caused me to grow; my prayer is that for others, reading it will have the same effect.

ACKNOWLEDGMENTS

Because of the nature of this work, it is not possible to name those who played such an important part in its preparation, but special thanks must be given to those who so faithfully encouraged me: the special women who read and commented on the various chapters, and those who so willingly shared their stories so that the material would have a depth beyond my own.

My deepest gratitude, however, goes to those very special men who allowed themselves to be used of God to assure me of my worth as a person and to motivate and assist me in completing the task set before me.

I WANT TO SCREAM

I want to scream because I was just a young
infant when he struck deep within my soul
I want to scream because I was so young when
he forced me to become a woman before I
had time to be a child
I want to scream because he rendered me
helpless
vulnerable
and trapped

I want to scream because he molested me in a
home that was built to protect me
I want to scream because he robbed me of my
childhood
my education
my laughter
and my beautiful smile

I want to scream because I feel like something
was frozen in the middle of my childhood
that the rest of me had grown, but that part of
me
which was I, myself, had never reached
adulthood

I want to scream because he confined me to a
world of silence and secrecy, solitude,
darkness and paralyzing fear
I want to scream because of all the years of pain
and harm I've caused myself, because the
pain was so great

I want to scream because of all the years I
minimized,

11

and I rationalized the abuse,
  because I thought no one would believe me
I want to scream because of all the harm he's
  done to me; the broken bones, for a child I
  may never have and for a past I'll never
  forget

I want to scream because the parents I wanted
  never were and never can be
I want to scream because I thought something
  was wrong with me, when it was with them

I want to scream because they repeatedly told me
  I was bad, no good and useless
  and would end up nowhere
  and I eventually believed them

I want to scream because the people who said
  they loved me only used me and now struggle
  to deny and cover the abuse
They instead have turned on me implying that I
  am sick, crazy, or disturbed to make such an
  accusation

I want to scream because the parents God gave
  to protect me
  I now am forced to abandon to survive

I want to scream because I want all to know
  that I am . . .
  a survivor of the quiet horror of incest.

—Written by Warren, 1986

a HOUSE DIVIDED

CHAPTER ONE

The Why of
It All

The throbbing pain was relentless. Every movement brought a sharp reminder of the swelling, spreading, scarlet-hued infection on her inner thigh. It finally brought Annie to the doctor's office. Later, she jokingly remarked, "I wouldn't even let him look at it until he put his hands behind his back." The diagnosis was a carbuncle infecting one of the more sensitive portions of her anatomy. The inflammation was totally distracting, but it was a mere blemish compared to the pain she carried in her heart.

Annie ultimately allowed the doctor to treat her physical distress and was soon cured. The other pain she has carried for more than twenty years. Even she does not examine it. I was allowed to glimpse it briefly, just once.

Annie is now almost forty years old. Her marriage finally disintegrated into divorce after seventeen painful years. For those years she endured physical beatings, demeaning verbal tirades, and the knowledge that her children were being physically abused by their father. She suspected sexual abuse, but lacked the courage to investigate that possibility. Her lot in life, she thought, was what she deserved. Her endurance reached its limits only when her husband was found, in a drunken rage, trying to strangle one of their daughters.

In the years since the separation from her husband,
she has taken into her bed more men than she would
care to number, regardless of their age or character. She
is attractive, their names are legion, and not one of them
has been able to provide the fulfillment she so desperately seeks. Her low self-image provides no permanent
attraction, as it often finds its expression in vile temper.
Each "lover" in turn has rejected her, adding to the
burden of her sense of worthlessness.

In an effort to escape her own reputation, she has
repeatedly moved from one section of town to another,
only to rebuild (often within weeks) what she has just
fled. She finally moved to another state, but her self-
defeating behavior caused her to choose a location near
an "old boyfriend"—and so begins again the cycle that
must eventually destroy her unless it can be interrupted. Surprisingly, she has high personal moral standards, and in constantly violating them she approaches
each day the point of total emotional annihilation. Yet,
her behavior is not unusual for many with her background.

Annie comes from an incestuous family. She is my
sister. We come from a house divided.

These pages will tell Annie's story, and they will tell
mine, but they will go far beyond that. They will tell the
story of thousands of victims; for while every story of
incest is unique to the individuals involved, many
threads bind them together in a common web of
bondage.

This book was almost never written. The past had
been settled and forgiven, and the offense no longer
needed rehearsal. Of all of the goals of my life, digging
through the past for the rusting razors of pain was not a
consideration. I was certainly not willing to commit the
story to publication.

My attention was first attracted by an article in *Time*

magazine entitled, "Cradle-to-Grave Intimacy." My revulsion turned to horror as I read:

> Wardell Pomeroy, co-author of the original Kinsey reports, says incest "can be sometimes beneficial" to children.[1]

Scarcely an inch lower on the page was a statement that caused my blood pressure to rise by several points:

> One conventional argument is that the fuss raised by parents after adult-child sex—and not the sex itself—is what harms the child.[2]

The authors of the "conventional arguments" had obviously not talked to very many victims.

The article redeems itself in the last quarter by quoting several professionals who are strongly opposed to such a view. The conclusion, a quotation from psychiatrist Edward Ritvo, says, "Childhood sexuality is like playing with a loaded gun."[3]

Rising social awareness had declared war on my self-enforced silence, but I was not about to surrender after the first skirmish. Aspirin, coffee, and single-minded concentration on a totally unrelated writing project enabled me to force the subject out of my conscious awareness. Three months later the battle was renewed, an attack in the form of an article which appeared in *Newsweek* magazine.

The very first paragraph of the article, entitled "An Epidemic of Incest," jarred my sleeping awareness of the problem to full military attention:

> Freud recoiled when his probing of human souls touched on incest, and his conclusion that child seduction was mainly fantasy may have helped keep society's secret for a few additional decades. But in the past year or two ... scholars project that one of every 100 adult

women in the United States was sexually molested as a child by her father. . . .[4]

The article was directed as positively as it is possible to present such a subject, I suppose. It revealed not only the existing problems, but the fact that, at least in some areas of the country, help is available. Its effect on me, however, was devastating. Aspirin and coffee, this time, were pointless. Visibly shaken, I started to walk. Several hours and many miles later I returned home, physically exhausted. Sleep, nonetheless, would not come easily that night, and when it did arrive, it was troubled. In the morning I resolutely picked up my own peace regarding the matter and hugged it close. I would not revive the issue another time. But I found that, somehow, there were now some uncomfortably rough edges to that precious peace, edges that I had not noticed before.

Wars are not won or lost in a single battle, but the decisive conflict is often more a matter of timing than of overt power of men and weapons. In January, I was presented with a rare gift of an evening to myself. During that evening the third and final attack was launched. It was perfectly directed.

As editor of the church's cassette library, I decided to indulge myself completely and "edit," during this relaxing interlude, a speaker whom I enjoyed, rather than having to be alert for theological discrepancies and/or poor programming. I settled on the sofa with a sewing project, anticipating a delightful time. The subject was biblical love and the need for personal involvement in the lives of others, even when that involvement entails personal discomfort, embarrassment or risk. The illustration was that of a young woman trapped in an incestuous relationship with her father.

Her cries for help, even to her pastor, had been totally ignored.

The sewing project I had planned for the evening lay untouched in my lap. Had the speaker and I been in his office, alone and face to face, he could not have commanded more of my attention. Too well I knew of what he spoke: the unheeded cries for help, the guilt and shame and denial, the overwhelming sense of violation that invades every portion of the incest victim's being. But I knew more than that. I knew that there was a way out of that maze of despair, and I knew that I was doing nothing to help those who were wandering helplessly in their own dilemma of degradation. I was no better than those in the illustration who had turned away from cries for help.

Still I was reluctant, and numerous excuses immediately came to mind to release me from the moral obligation that appeared unbidden before me. Almost every person involved in my story is alive and very important to me. Discovery that I made the innermost secrets of our family a matter of public scrutiny, even under assumed names, would most certainly cause severance from the very people I sought to draw closer. Discovery of their identity by others would cause mischief just as great, if not greater. The price of incest discovered includes social and emotional ostracism, even when that discovery is thirty years after the fact.

When I compared the possibility of pain to the few with the known factors of agony for the many victims, however, there was no real choice. The white flag of surrender was raised. As you read, I ask you to remember that this story ends in love. Often that will seem to be an impossibility, but without love as its culmination, the story could never have been written at all.

This is not a "nice little book" filled with spiritual platitudes to be read on a quiet Sunday afternoon. Read it when you will; parts of it are quite ugly. Incest is a problem that tends to reverberate not only through an entire life, but through the generations that proceed from it as well. My own story was not complete until recent months. The acts of incest performed thirty years ago have not yet ceased to bear their evil fruit in all of the lives concerned. Help cannot be given to those who are unwilling to face the problem, and there are many who cannot bear to uncover their wounds.

Instead of platitudes, I offer understanding and a course of action. If you become one of those who is willing to hold out a helping hand and an open heart to those who have been victimized, then all that I have had to exhume to write these pages will have been worth it. But it is not primarily to the potential "helpers" that I direct this book.

I write this book for the Annies and the Katies of this world. I know your pain, for I have borne it myself, but I also know a road which leads to healing and peace. There is a sense in which we can never be completely whole. Something has been taken from us which can never be replaced, as if an arm had been amputated, or a foot. We can forgive and adjust, but it will be gone forever. We can, however, learn to accept what has happened and lead lives of fullness and joy, of trust and freedom from the ghosts that would haunt our sleep . . . and we can insure that the homes that we build will not perpetrate the crime that has been committed against us.

CHAPTER TWO

Annie and Me

> *You did not come ...*
> *You love not me.*
>
> Thomas Hardy
> *A Broken Appointment*

Once, when I was grown, a neighbor boy, eight or nine years old, brought me his tangled kite string. Challenged by the task, and charmed by the pleading in his eyes (and his faith in me to accomplish the feat), I set to unravelling his near-copy of the Gordian knot. After an hour's labor, undertaken with much patience, the mass had been drastically reduced, but there still remained one lump of such intrinsic complexity that my perseverance failed. Moving to my sewing box, I brought out my scissors. The small head nodded assent, and I cut the knot. As I tied the two good ends together into a smaller, more manageable union, the problem was solved. With the ends cut, the remaining problem knot was easy to untangle. We discovered that we had lost only fourteen inches of valuable kite string.

Life's entanglements are not quite that easy to undo. The deficiencies and hurts of one generation are too often transmitted to the next, and, undealt with, they seem to breed deficiency and pain equal to or exceeding their own. One can sometimes trace causes and effects, but all too often, important information is missing from the total picture and all seems hopelessly entwined, never to be fully unwound or understood.

Yet life is not inexorably determined by the past. It often helps to know the events and attitudes that have caused the circumstances of our lives, but knowing the past is not imperative for determining the future. We all must come to the place of deciding for ourselves which road we will travel. Sometimes we may find that we must reach for a helping hand in order to leave the path that has been worn deep by the others who have gone before us—but we can leave it.

Incest is not a problem that began yesterday. The seeds of the disordered family situation which allow for incest usually send forth their shoots only after they have lain in poisoned soil through a generation or more. In order to understand the total effect of my incest, we must travel briefly to a previous age: the time when my parents were young and struggling with the issues of their world.

Mother's family was overturned while she was in her early teens by the death of my grandmother. Devastated by the loss, my grandfather sought to drown his grief in alcohol. Wandering in a continual haze of befuddled intoxication, he lost touch with his responsibilities toward his two daughters. Lacking parental support and guidance, my mother sought consolation in the arms of successive boyfriends. At seventeen she met my father, who came from a different but equally destructive household.

John, who would become my father, came from a matriarchal home. Grandma ruled with a heavily accented voice of iron; her major purpose in life was, apparently, insuring that neither she nor any member of her family would ever depend on an outside agency for sustenance. That concept included a healthy balance in a savings account. The man she had married, however, lacked motivation for anything beyond the minimal comforts of life. Papa was content with his pipe in his hand and his children at his feet. Constantly goaded to an achievement beyond his power to attain, he retreated behind his newspaper to a private world, to an escape from the voices that would give him no rest.

Grandma went out to work, turning household responsibilities over to Marge, the oldest child. Less than ten years old, Marge relished her position, and her authority over her two younger siblings, John and Molly. She never relinquished her power, and John resented her deeply.

A genius by psychologists' definitions, John knew by the time he was in eighth grade that he wanted to become a civil engineer. Grandma and Marge shared a more immediate economy, however, and refused to support his education beyond age fifteen. Untrained for more sophisticated employment, he found a job as a delivery boy for a grocery store. At sixteen he carried bricks for a construction crew. At seventeen he wearied of contributing to the support of a family that would not even consider his desires, and took refuge instead in the arms of the woman who became my mother. They were physically and emotionally too young, but they married anyway. I was born a year later, two weeks before my mother's eighteenth birthday. Despite their youth and the problems of immaturity, they were able to provide a world of love and relative security for me—until I was four.

Then Daddy went away for what seemed a long time, and when he came back he was dressed in khaki. Almost before I realized his arrival, he was gone again. This time, I was told, he would not be back so soon. The United States had entered World War II. I began to wait. They told me that a new baby was coming to our

23

house, and I would stay with Aunt Marge until it arrived. Annie was born in September. She was beautiful.

Marge was married to Al. Defense work often kept him away from home, and he appeared only as a shadowy recollection in my early memories. Impatient, fiery-tempered, and strong-willed, he simply did not enter into the equation of my life until I was eleven years old—as the perpetrator of my incest.

Al had come from a deprived home. His parents had farmed land that was more suited for the raising of stones than edible crops, and they succumbed early to the strain of rearing ten children on such barren ground. As the ninth of the ten, Al was sent to live with an older sister. No amount of coercion will induce him to discuss his experiences there. Only a blue stream of curses expresses his hatred.

The one bright spot in my life at Marge's house was Papa. Small and quiet, he never varied the ceremony of his coming home from work. It was our time together, to the exclusion of all others. I lived for that portion of the day when his footsteps could be heard coming down the hall. To him belonged my giddy laughter and unrestrained four-year-old kisses; in exchange, he gave steady love and the quiet security of his arms. But the laughter stilled before I was five, and the security was stolen away. They took him to the hospital during the night. A few days later, the man who made my life bearable was dead.

I screamed my rage, and I cried until there were no more tears, but nobody held me. It was good that they didn't try, because I wouldn't have let them. They weren't sufficient for my grief.

Then the funeral was over. Time resumed its march through the days of my life. The slashing pain of parting became the dull ache that could only be shared by one other, my father—and he was gone. I waited. They had told me I could go home "after the new baby comes." The new baby was three months old. "When your mother is stronger." She got strong enough to get a job. "After your Daddy comes home from war." I went to kindergarten and learned how to skip and play "A Tisket a Tasket," and then I went to first grade and learned how to read. But those were secondary occupations. The thing I was most concerned with was waiting.

Marge didn't like me, not the way Papa had, or my mother. She never touched me—except to wash me, as if there were some vile spot that could be removed only by drawing forth wails of protest; or to comb my "stringy" hair, not caring if she pulled until I cried. She never kissed me the way she did Annie, who had come to live with us. That was all right. I didn't belong in Marge's house anyway—I belonged with my mother. Grandma was nice, and so was Molly, but they were at work all day. I asked about home until they no longer even bothered to hear the question.

My introduction to the sexual side of life began when I was six. There had been a series of child abductions that year in our city. Both at school and at home I received dire warnings about taking candy or rides from strange men. Nobody ever told me what would happen if I disobeyed, but I knew from the tone of what was said that disobedience was not an option.

The four-block walk from school was short enough even for my six-year-old legs, and the "shortcut" through the alleyway made the journey even more convenient. One afternoon, while the weather was still warm, I was meandering home from school at the end of the day, kicking a pebble to watch it bounce across the bricks of the alley floor. A man at the other end of the alley faced the garage doors. As I approached, he turned. Trousers open at the fly, he was fully exposed.

More shocking than the sight of his flesh, however, was the leering grin on his face. I took flight and covered the block that remained to Marge's house in record time.

No one was home, although the door was open for me. Shaking, I locked both the screen door and the inner door and then cried myself to sleep on the sofa. I was awakened by Marge, shaking me angrily. Having been locked out of her house, she was demanding to know the reason. But it was too late—there was already too much distance between us. She had been locked out of my life more certainly than she had been locked out of the house, and the probability of her gaining entrance was considerably more remote. I told her that I didn't know.

Frightening as the incident was, I might have dismissed and forgotten it apart from what happened the following spring in the same alleyway. Another man joined me on my walk through the narrow passage. Cheerful, and obviously interested in what I had to say, he at first gave me no cause for fear. His move was sudden, and I found myself trembling and embarrassed, backed into a niche between garages. Pushing at the hem of my dress he asked, ". . . just let me see your panties." I resisted, and the man changed his approach. Releasing me he offered to "buy an ice-cream cone." The warnings rang clear in my memory. Knowing that the only way out of the alley was past Marge's house, I agreed. As we passed the gate, I made a frantic dash into the yard, telling my would-be "benefactor" that I would have to ask permission from my aunt. He did not deter me.

Marge was visiting a neighbor. Again, I was alone. Again I locked all the doors, and again fell asleep on the sofa. In shame and humiliation, fearing to reveal the cause for my action, I again kept silence. This time I was spanked for my behavior. I had learned not to trust strange men. But there was never any warning about the dangers that lurked within the walls of my own home.

Then Daddy came back. I'd waited so long, and it was so good to have him hold me and hug me again.

"Now we can go home to Mommy."

"Not yet. Wait a little while." I backed away from him, tears streaming down my face.

"Why? You said . . ."

"Mommy still has to work for a little while until I can find a job. When Mommy doesn't work anymore, then you can come home . . ."

". . . Maybe." When I was eight years old my parents were divorced. Nobody ever told me. I overheard it in a conversation concerning custody for Annie and me.

One thing was obvious to my eight-year-old reasoning—my parents didn't want me anymore. I didn't want Marge, and I suspected that the feeling was mutual, but Annie was mine—she was my sister. From the day of her birth she had been like some large, beautiful, animated baby doll to me. I could imagine no greater perfection. Nearly five years' difference in our ages made little difference to me, and if I sometimes resented having to stay in the yard to "watch Annie," it was only a minor irritation. I loved her without reservation until the day that she herself shattered the image I had of her. That story began shortly after I turned nine.

Daddy came over to talk to Marge and Al. They were seated around the kitchen table, and I, on the floor with some paper dolls, paid little attention to their conversation. Then Marge's voice raised irritably.

"We'll find a good home for the other one."

"No." My father's voice was firm. "I won't split them up. If you want Annie, you'll have to take Katie, too."

I left the cut-out figures on the floor and quietly went outside. We were going to be adopted. I didn't want that. I wanted my own parents, not Marge, who was always complaining about me. But then, nobody asked me what I wanted.

Summer came and Daddy got married again. Maybe he would change his mind and let us live with him. Maybe the adoption would be forgotten. And then he told me.

"You know that when you are adopted you can't call me 'Daddy' anymore."

"But you are my daddy."

"After the adoption, Al will be your daddy."

"I want you."

"I know, but that can't be."

"What about Annie?"

"Her, too."

"What will I call you?"

"Uncle John."

I didn't let him see me cry.

The social worker came to the house with a lot of papers and more questions. Annie and I had been scrubbed and polished, and when we were asked if we wanted Marge and Al to be our parents, we both gave an enthusiastic "yes." I'd already lost too much; I wasn't going to lose Annie, too.

The court date arrived. Marge wondered aloud whether my mother would care enough to show up. She didn't. Neither did "Uncle" John. Wearing identical outfits, Annie and I stood with Marge and Al at the judge's bench. Annie's particular attractiveness was radiant that day, and the judge plucked her out of Al's arms and placed her on his own lap. Opening the top drawer of his bench, he allowed her to choose a packet of sweets. After a few adoring comments regarding Annie, and some praise for Marge and Al concerning the wonderful thing they were doing, the judge glanced at me. "Her, too?"

"Yes."

"Petition granted."

In the hallway outside of the courtroom, the lawyer explained to my "new parents" that birth certificates would be altered according to customary procedures, and copies forwarded to them. I guessed that sometimes it was all right to lie if you were an adult.

Marge wondered about my mother. The lawyer continued, "Of course, she can't see them until they have reached eighteen." Eighteen! Eighteen was a lifetime as far as I was concerned. But I would wait.

Then we were outside. "Annie, can I have a piece of your candy?"

"No."

"Please?"

"NO! He gave it to ME." Her smile was evil.

"Katie, stop it!" Marge was still busy with the lawyer and irritated by the distraction I was causing.

I tried to play with Annie in the car on the way home, but it just wasn't the same anymore. No matter what I did, she whined. Finally, Marge reached back and swatted me across the arm.

"Stop picking on her; you'll make her sick."

I was the one who was sick. My beautiful baby sister had turned into a greedy little monster before my eyes. The reason for my agreement to the adoption crumbled before the paperwork had been completed. I was isolated from the last person whom I had loved, and it would be years before the breach would begin to heal.

We decided to call Al "Daddy," but it never occurred to either of us to call Marge "Mom." I waited for my real mother to call on my eighteenth birthday. She didn't. Nor did she call in the months that followed. Only then did I toss her title, the leftover remnant of a hope unfulfilled, to Marge, much as one tosses the scraps of a meal to a family pet. I simply didn't care anymore.

"Daddy" meant little more to me after the adoption

than he did before. The relationship between him and Annie was special; she would sit on his lap by the hour being read to or watching television. Marge, too, had her special times with my sister, and I can still picture Annie seated on the floor in front of Marge having her thick, glossy hair brushed dry. Not consciously jealous of either relationship, I did not believe that their love was particularly important to me. I wanted to go back to where I belonged. The only problem was that the place I longed for no longer existed.

The summer after the adoption proceedings we moved into a newly-built house in the suburbs. In September I entered a different school. We didn't live with relatives anymore; it was just the four of us. Daddy and Marge argued a lot, in words which I was forbidden to use. Usually, I could maintain a low profile and stay out of the way of vile tempers, but the stage was being set for my drama of horrors.

The sad fact of any form of child abuse, whether it be physical, emotional or sexual, is that the abused become the abusers. Both my natural parents and my stepparents had suffered either abuse or deprivation in one form or another during childhood. Such abuse, combined with marital difficulties, was bound to seek ventilation in anger and frustration. Sexual abuse is undoubtedly caused by anger and frustration, not the desire for sexual gratification. My stepparents' poor impulse control, demonstrated by violent tempers and verbal ravishment, was another indication that there was danger ahead.

Feelings of isolation and rejection, along with an alienation from my mother (the surrogate who fills that vacancy is relatively unimportant), almost predisposed me to sexual victimization. The two incidents with the men in the alley would not have changed if family relationships had been different, but the outcome of fear and withdrawal might have been. Coping skills could have developed from those experiences which would have served me in future confrontations.

As things were, the only wonder is that my victimization didn't occur sooner.

CHAPTER THREE

Demise of Innocence

> *The Soul has Bandaged moments—*
> *When too appalled to stir—*
> *She feels some ghastly Fright come up*
> *And stop to look at her—*

> Emily Dickinson

We became an isolated family. With the exception of a few relatives, outsiders were rarely guests in our home. Until I left home some nine years later, there was never an instance when someone unrelated sat down at the dinner table with us. The assortment of friends who had drifted in and out of the household in my younger days totally disappeared. Though there were a few instances of our visiting, and some summer excursions that brought us together with Marge's friends, once the adoption took place these, too, became less and less frequent. Life was punctuated with family quarrels, vile language, and criticism. Yet those factors would seem like havens of safety compared to the events that followed just two years after the adoption proceedings.

The summer that I finished the sixth grade, one of Daddy's brothers came to visit from out of town. His family consisted of two girls near my sister's age and a seventeen-year-old son, Jack. While the adults talked upstairs and Annie went into the playroom with the young girls, Jack and I went down to the family room and danced to some records. He was handsome by any standards, and I was flattered by the attentions of someone who was nearly six years my senior.

After we had danced for a while, he asked if I had ever "done it." The moral standards at the school that I attended left something to be desired, so in spite of my youth and naïveté I had at least a vague idea of what he was talking about, though I lacked a concrete definition of "it." I confessed my innocence.

His line was smooth, at least from my eleven-year-old point of view; he was experienced, and he had just about convinced me to experiment. As he exposed himself, however, I had a sudden flashback to the face of the man in the alley. Almost numb with horror, I turned and fled. The evening was at an end, and as I stood in the backyard waiting for my pounding heart to calm down, I vowed that I would never again be "smooth-talked" into something over which I had such serious doubts. I was flushed with guilt and shame.

About a month after the incident with Jack, the family room was converted into a bar where Daddy could entertain his customers. Having opened a small real estate office some months before, he felt that some of his contacts required special attention. A display case was built into the room, designed especially to hold a collection of small, hand-carved figurines that he had acquired over the years. Deciding to protect the figures with lacquer before putting them into the case, he drafted me to help with the job of unpacking them from their storage boxes and dipping them into their protective bath.

It was summer, and the last thing I wanted to do was spend an evening in the basement dipping figurines. Many of them were obscene and embarrassing, and I really didn't care to spend a whole evening dodging

33

Daddy's caustic temper. I was still young enough to prefer trying to catch some of the fireflies that had been seen in the neighborhood that summer. My plans were to fill a jar with enough fireflies to provide illumination for reading after the lights were turned out at night. Daddy insisted, however, and I complied. I was mildly surprised at his comparatively gentle reaction to my whining complaint.

The job seemed endless. Each figurine had been individually wrapped before packing it into one of several cardboard cases. Despite his apparently genial mood, I lived in dread of a temperamental outburst each time that I was slow or clumsy. There was a reward, however. For my labors he prepared a drink for me. Not Coke or cherry soda or ginger ale, but real liquor and white soda. "Our little secret," he said, and my excitement was kindled at the prospect of being able to do such a "grown-up" thing.

The second "cocktail" didn't taste quite as good as the first, but the thought of "our little secret" was enough to help me to finish it. When he offered the third drink, I refused. My head was getting light and my stomach was making mild objection to the alcohol. He insisted, and rather than risk his temper, I finally agreed. "Unfortunately," the bottle of white soda was empty, and he sent me to the refrigerator in the next room to fetch another. With my head spinning slightly, I obeyed. He followed me.

"Here, let me give you a little kiss for helping me," he whispered. My nightmare had begun. This was not the quick peck on the cheek that Annie and I had been accustomed to at bedtime. His arms went around me, he held me very close, and his tongue forced its way between my lips. It was the kind of action that the girls talked about at school during recess, the kind of kiss associated with "necking." My body stiffened in resistance. "It's okay," he assured me. But it was not, and I knew it.

Pressing me against the refrigerator, his hand reached under my jersey and he began to fondle my breasts. Resistance turned to terror. My repeated pleas of "No, no," were met with, "Just a little." When I began to panic and cry, he released me.

"Now, sit down and take it easy for a few minutes," he ordered. I obeyed. The third drink was prepared for me, and while I stared numbly into the glass he tried to reassure me. "It's okay. It was just a little kiss. It's okay for a man to kiss his daughter, isn't it?" The question demanded at least a nod. "All right now," he instructed as I managed to force the now-bitter liquid down my throat, "go upstairs and get into bed so Marge doesn't know you've been drinking. Remember, this is our little secret." Guilty over the forbidden drinks, bewildered over the obvious conflict in his statements, and frightened by his seductive behavior, I did as he told me.

School opened for the fall semester. I was now a seventh grader. Life began another cycle, for the most part much the same as all of the other cycles before, only nothing would ever be quite the same again. I was different.

One of the most popular girls in my class began to show an interest in television wrestling. Longing for an acceptance which I had never experienced, I too developed an "interest" in the theatrics of the sport. Daddy noticed and asked if I would like to attend a wrestling match as my birthday present. He had repeated his "embraces" several times since the night in the basement and I was afraid to be alone with him at home. At least being "out" with him seemed to offer some protection by measure of the presence of others.

I don't remember being particularly impressed with the atmosphere and the noise, but when he told me to go forward to the ring to get autographs, I did so. Close-up contact with the personalities and the odors of the sport were quite enough to cure me of any aspirations to match my schoolmate's interest. I never watched another match, live or televised.

Then the wrestling matches began at home. Acceptable as "play" even in Marge's presence, they afforded him opportunity not only to touch every part of my body, but to place me in "holds" that made me squirm with their sexual intent. From time to time Annie would try to join the forays, but she was only a minor distraction to his real purpose. After a few minutes of play, she would either turn aside to another interest, or be called away by Marge so that she "wouldn't get hurt." My interest in television wrestling was long dead, but there seemed no way to avoid the almost daily matches on the living room floor.

Marge joined a bowling league. The arguments between her and Daddy had increased in both frequency and intensity, and the league afforded her an opportunity for a "night out with the girls." Daddy was left to babysit; I, at age twelve, was not deemed equal to caring for my seven-year-old sister. The assumption was probably well justified, as we often engaged in some rather violent verbal battles. "Bowling night" was Tuesday. Before leaving the house, Marge would tuck Annie into bed upstairs. That left me alone, downstairs with Daddy.

Marge wasn't out of the house for twenty minutes when I was commanded to take a seat on the sofa beside my stepfather. This time his explorations went further. My pleas, "No, no," were again ignored as his hand slid under my waistband. "It's all right, just a little bit" was his answer—it became his standard phrase for the next eighteen months. After what seemed an eternity, I was finally released from his unwelcome embrace. I went to bed immediately, my heart pounding with confusion and fear.

Each week the routine was repeated, the exploration, the liberties taken often just a bit beyond what had happened the week before. In desperation, I began to plead tiredness on Tuesday nights, often following Annie to bed within minutes. I hated going to bed at 7:00, but my feigned weariness seemed to provide a measure of safety. Even the wrestling matches seemed to diminish in number, and for several weeks Daddy didn't touch me. Once Marge started to question me about Tuesdays, but did not pursue my casual, "I don't know."

Actually, Annie and I had a lot of fun on those nights. Since she wasn't sleeping when I came to bed, we often made up games and fantasies which made it difficult to stifle giggles. She cooperated because our antics delayed the time when she would have to sleep. After an hour or so, we would both drift off. Life seemed more secure, but it was a fragile security, built on wishes rather than effective defensive actions.

I was awakened from my sleep and my pseudo-security all too soon. Daddy moved into my bed. "Shh, you'll wake Annie." Surely, one could not take the risk of waking Annie, and so I remained silent. Without actual penetration, he went through all of the motions of the sex act while tears streamed down my face and I bit my lip until it bled.

Finally there came what seemed like some real relief from my dilemma. I was asked to accept a regular baby-sitting job on Tuesday evenings. It was an immediate cure for my Tuesday night weariness. Not only did I love the two little boys I was to care for, but the job was to last until 10:30. Marge usually arrived home by 11:00. I almost trembled with relief, not realizing how short-lived it would be.

The air seemed particularly sweet as I walked the short distance to my assignment. The two-year-old was already in bed, but the four-year-old was waiting for me to read a story. Later, as I tucked him into bed, I felt as safe as he did. It was a lovely, relaxed evening. When the parents arrived home at the promised time, I was undisturbed. There would be no time for Daddy's attentions tonight.

Unknown to me, Marge had planned a party with her team for that evening. As I walked into the living room I saw Daddy, seated on the sofa, wearing nothing but his cranberry-colored dressing gown. It was a "no holds barred" night, stopping just short of the ultimate in humiliation. As his fingers probed the interior portions of my body I was frantic, afraid, and powerless to tell anybody what was happening.

The following Tuesday my mouth was dry as I walked home. Not only had the week before destroyed the confidence that I had found the solution to my problem, but my employers had come home thirty minutes early. I heard voices as I walked into the house, and an unexpected wave of relief swept over me. As I turned the corner into the living room I saw a neighbor, a friend of Daddy's. I didn't like the man. Visiting his home had often involved some uncomfortable "touching." Although there was nothing overtly sexual about it, there was an implied intimacy that made me uneasy. Tonight, he looked like an angel in disguise. He proved to be an agent of mortification.

When Daddy demanded that I stand before him, I reluctantly complied. I didn't think that he would molest me in front of anyone else, but there was something in his voice. He wrestled me to the floor and pinned my shoulders with his buttocks. The fly of his trousers rested against my face. One thin layer of clothing separated me from my ultimate threat. I felt totally exposed. The ugly laughter and leering faces that accompanied my agony as I frantically turned my head aside sealed a hatred in my heart, a hatred that would remain there for more than twenty years.

I am constantly amazed at the degree of naïveté and sophistication that can exist in a person at the same time. I knew what sex was for, but I had no idea of "how far" one had to go before pregnancy resulted. I had only the information gained from schoolmates who, despite much "talk," were almost as uninformed as I. Several months after Daddy's first "approach" to me, my first menstrual period began. It did not reappear for six months. After the third month, I stood daily before the full-length mirror, wondering if I were pregnant. Having no real confidantes, I could ask no one the explicit questions which plagued me. Searching all of the printed material available to me concerning sexual matters, I found that they, too, stopped short of the things I really needed to know.

After my fourth month of "wondering," Marge took me to the doctor. The emotions that raced through my heart were multiple. "What if I *were* pregnant?" "If he discovered what was happening, what would be the result?" "Would he believe me if I said it was Daddy?" Without a physical examination, the physician simply explained that the irregularity was a very common occurrence. He grinned, winked, and said, "Of course, you haven't been fooling around with the boys, have you?"

"No." I flushed, but my heart continued inwardly, "Only with Daddy." My fear of pregnancy continued for another two months.

Early in November of my thirteenth year, Daddy made a move toward copulation. I had endured his fondling of my body. I had gritted my teeth as his fingers explored the most private parts of my being. I

39

fought nausea as he thrust his flesh between my thighs. I had endured all that I could endure; the limitations of my tolerance had been reached. As I begged him to stop, my pleas were again met with "Just a little" and "Just once." Terror overcame all other considerations, and I finally dared to physically resist him. Neither one of us had realized the strength I was capable of, but it was a strength born of determination and fear.

Later, lying in bed, both longing for sleep and dreading it, I knew that there could be no "next time." I spent a long night considering the alternatives.

I had been sent to Sunday school and church with regularity and was in the second year of a two-year course of study for acceptance into the church as a member. The catechism served only to increase my sense of guilt and shame. Fear finally overcame those feelings, and one Saturday morning I lingered until the other students had departed. After some stumbling and several false starts, I blurted out to my pastor, "My father tried to rape me."

If I had announced that I had leprosy, he could not have been more repulsed. His lip curled as he turned away from me. The brief reply to my revelation indicated that since my experience was past tense, I need not worry. As I tried to explain that my danger was very immediate, he cut me off. "Everything will be all right," he assured me. My courage in coming to him had been completely wasted.

Fortunately, two changes worked together to prevent any further advances. First of all, Marge decided to leave the bowling team. Although very few lives were ever lived to her satisfaction, her criticism of the team members had been particularly severe. The holiday season offered a convenient excuse for her departure. Secondly, my eighth-grade teacher decided to have personal conferences with each student in his class.

One student was scheduled for a "private talk" each night after school. My appointment was the last one before Christmas vacation.

"Popularity" had never been a descriptive term which could be applied to me with any degree of accuracy. As I talked with my teacher, I at first blamed my lack of successful peer relationships on the fact that I wanted to be with my natural mother. As we continued talking, however, I finally confessed the real source of my problem—Daddy. My teacher sat in shocked silence. When I was able to relate that I felt relatively safe during the Christmas season because of Marge's presence in the house he relaxed somewhat, but he promised to resume our discussion when school began again in January. It had been dark for a considerable time when I left the building that night.

Holidays are busy for thirteen-year-olds. People require baby-sitters with great frequency, and it seemed that during the weeks that school was out I was coming in late three or four times each week. Between Christmas and the New Year I had one engagement that led to another early the next morning. It was late when I came home, and Marge and Daddy had already gone upstairs to bed. As I did not have an alarm clock, it was necessary for me to ask Marge to wake me in the morning. Turning the corner into their bedroom I noticed that both of them were in the same twin bed. Relating my request as quickly as I could, I turned and left the room, elated. I was certain that I was free! Reasoning that if he were having sex with Marge, Daddy would no longer disturb me, I almost danced my way to bed. The sleep disturbances so common to incest victims did not trouble me that night. There would be no unwelcome visitor in the dark—at least for a while.

Several days later I used some of my Christmas gift stationery to write to my teacher. Informing him that there was no more need for worry because of my "important discovery," I folded the note and placed it between the covers of my school loose-leaf binder. Singing in my new felt freedom, I took up the bird cage and disappeared into the basement to clean it, this time without a murmur of complaint. I had not been long at my work when Marge summoned me upstairs. She was standing in the kitchen, holding the newly written note. She demanded an explanation.

My incestuous "affair" was over. Some of the burdens that it had impressed upon me would be multiplied before the week was two days older. Those burdens of shame, guilt and a sense of complete worthlessness were all false burdens, common to incest victims, but I didn't know that.

There were other factors that I held in common with other incest victims, too, but like so many of them I didn't even realize that there were other victims. The comparatively mild beginnings of our hidden relationship, Daddy's justifications, the subtle progression of the affair, and my own youthful inability to reason through the situation in a logical manner had all worked to render useless the few coping abilities that I possessed. Obedience was the only road I knew to safety from conflict, and except for minor issues, I was always obedient. This had clearly been no minor issue.

CHAPTER FOUR

Aftermath

> *Shame need not crouch*
> *In such an Earth as*
> *Ours—*
> *Shame—stand erect—*
> *The Universe is yours.*
>
> Emily Dickinson

As I stood before Marge, I struggled with the two conflicting factors of obedience: Daddy's demand that I keep "our little secret," and Marge's demand to know. It was tempting to deny everything, to let "well enough alone." Language difficulties embarrassed me (despite the fact that I had already attempted to communicate my problem to two others), and the necessity of talking to Marge about sexual matters terrified me. My entire sex education had consisted of the "Kotex Book" tossed casually into my lap one evening when I was ten. At the same time, I wanted desperately to vent the anger and hatred that had built up within me during the past months. Any struggle was pointless. Marge would have the story, now, and in any language that I had at my command to communicate it.

"Daddy tried to rape me" was all that I could blurt out, my voice a fear-constricted whisper. I find it simply amazing, in light of the shocking nature of that revelation and the events that followed, that I was never once asked to elaborate on that simple statement. Fully thirty years passed before anyone ever heard the entire story.

Whatever my faults in Marge's eyes, she knew that I was not a liar. Within the hour she had made a decision to see a lawyer to "take care of it." As we were leaving the house, however, Daddy came home. When confronted with my accusation, he denied it and told Marge that if she would just take me to a doctor she would know that he was innocent. I was beaten, and I knew it. All of the humiliation, the fear, the repulsion that I had lived with had left me a virgin, technically. The Kotex book had taught me that much. At that moment I really didn't know if I hated him more for what he had done to me, or for what he had not done. At least if he had forced himself on me, completing the act, I would have had proof of his actions. As it was, I was left holding only my empty pain.

The trip to the doctor was made, a doctor that had never been seen by the family before. Without explanation or apology I was made to expose myself to this stranger, and when he had finished his work I was summarily dismissed to the waiting room. Marge joined me about twenty minutes later. The doctor never saw me again. He hadn't spoken one word to me. I was dehumanized, and any ability that I had to stand in my own defense was melting away like an April snow.

In the car on the way home, Marge repeated the doctor's explanation to her. This was all, most likely, a product of my "imagination." Such accusations were not uncommon, and often followed guilt over masturbation or sexual contact with some boy. I thought of Jack and knew that my case was weakening. I would press the issue no further. I would not lie; I would simply refuse to insist.

The pastor was called in, and after some conferences

behind closed doors with my parents, they left the room. The pastor wanted to speak to me. He gently patted me on the shoulder and told me that it would be best just to forget the incident. "Incident," however, was never defined. I will never know if he referred to the violation of my body or the disclosure of that violation. He left the house.

Marge took me aside next. She explained quietly that since a marriage and a business were at stake, and she had only my word for the charges, the matter would be dropped. I would like to believe that she really didn't know, but the best that I can come up with is that her denial systems were very hard at work. In the family picture album there was a photograph of Daddy, Annie and myself, just two months earlier. The three of us stood in front of the house, Annie on Daddy's right side, his hand resting lightly on her shoulder, and I on his left—his hand cupping my left breast. Marge had snapped the shutter on the camera. If she had missed the significance of that picture, it is difficult to believe that she had missed the significance of the diary that she made me destroy. I had kept it over the course of the previous year, and she read it while I left the house to go to the grocery store for cookies—an item which seldom made an appearance in our home.

After Marge's decision, Daddy called me into the spare room. "Let's just forget all of this" was all that he would say. Then he put his arms around me and kissed me. It was like the night in the basement all over again. I stood there, passive, but I felt the bile rise up into my throat. After the events of the past forty-eight hours I was too broken to resist physically. Mentally, my attitude was quite different. If I could have killed him and gotten away with it, I would have. As it was, I turned and walked out of the room without comment the moment he released me.

The subject was never mentioned again by my parents, the pastor or the teacher at school. I decided to fight my own battles, to do things my own way. Submission to authority and truth had certainly done me no good at all. Being a "good little girl" had left me on the outside, looking in. I would become part of the "in" group. My parents would have to guess at what was really going on in my life. Morality had assumed a new shape. From now on, it would serve me.

The new semester began about a week later. I began by telling all the "important" girls what my stepfather had done. "He tried to rape me" was sufficient for them. As I became a part of their company, I adopted their habits and learned to smoke. It was not difficult and made me feel quite mature. I stole cigarettes from my parents, and when that could not be accomplished without detection, I stole the money needed to buy my own. Daddy saved coins in a box in his office safe. He usually did not lock the safe, but when he did, I knew how to gain access. Somehow, I knew just how much I could get away with without detection. He unwittingly supplied my needs for almost five years.

My third "accomplishment" was to get drunk. Invited to a pajama party with three of the most rebellious girls in the class, I shared with them the pint of whiskey and half-gallon of wine that they had managed to pilfer from their parents. The four of us consumed the alcohol within the space of two hours. Needless to say, we all became quite ill. The nausea, plus the realization that alcohol robbed me of full control of my faculties, cured me forever of any real enthusiasm for liquor.

Through the end of the first semester of eighth grade I had been an "A" student. My grades plummeted. "C's" and "D's" were the most I could manage during the rest of that year. They rose only slightly during my high school career. Counselor after counselor would call me into his office to tell me, "Katherine, you really can do so much better." I never bothered to answer; it wasn't worth the trouble.

Daddy initiated a couple of "deals" to help me. As a compulsive spender, no matter what I earned baby-sitting, I was always bereft of funds. In an effort to teach me to save, and also to help motivate me to raise my grades, he offered to pay into a savings account rewards for good grades, as well as matching any baby-sitting money that I would put aside. My rebellion was too deep to allow me to agree to any plan for which I could not claim immediate benefit. When he sealed each of the deals with one of his particular brand of kisses, I was determined to do as little as possible to cooperate. Only about one-fourth of the baby-sitting funds that should have been set aside ever found their way into his hands. If my grades merited any funds at all, it made little difference to me.

Personal hatred waxed strong. I bullied when I could get away with it, got even whenever I saw the chance. Daddy had a pocket watch that I had often admired. With little coercion he gave it to me to wear as a pendant. Within a week I deliberately broke it. For years, at least one piece of flatware at his place at the table was contaminated. Most often I would drop his spoon and step on it before putting it in place. There were no household jobs that I did willingly; those I completed were accomplished so badly that both parents soon despaired that I would ever be able to do anything properly, a fear that they widely advertised. Dishes were washed poorly and put away with drops of water still clinging to their surfaces. Ironing was always scorched, especially if my allotted portion included any of Daddy's undergarments. I avoided staying at home; my first job began on the day I became old enough to legally hold one.

Shortly after the furor of my disclosure died down, Grandma came to live with us. Demanding, disruptive and unbelievably stubborn in the lives of others, she became a refuge for me. She never knew what happened between Daddy and me, but she didn't need to. What she did know was that I needed support against Annie's "games," and she often came to my defense. She knew that when Marge called me fat I needed encouragement, and she could be counted on to come through with a remark about the "marvelous" way I did my hair. She knew that I couldn't stand up under Daddy's temper, and she would be available with enough tissue and the tenderness to dry my tears. Twice, when I stood in the ticket line at the bus depot, ready to run away from home, the thought of Grandma made me turn back.

Ninth grade meant the beginning of a new school. I still didn't seem to fit in, but it was better than before. Rebellion always seems to find company. I enjoyed most of my classes, especially English. The teacher was a model of patient understanding as she guided me through a mercifully short section in grammar, at which I was totally inept. Progressing to Greek mythology, I was fascinated with the material and my grades soared to undreamed-of heights. When we came to the writing section, I was eager.

We were assigned an essay describing a recent dream. Although I always dreamed frequently, nothing in particular came to mind, at least nothing that I wanted to commit to paper. I decided to make up a dream, one that I would like to have, one that would be sufficiently dramatic to merit the telling.

In the make-believe dream, I saw my natural mother dressed in ethereal blue gauze. Gracefully making her way toward me through an arbor of roses, she beckoned me to join her. Whether or not I was conscious that this was one more desperate cry for help I don't remember, but it was effective to that end. Within days, the teacher approached me about a conference. While the issue of rejoining my natural mother was still of primary importance to me, it was powerfully overshadowed by the events of the previous two years. I told her what Daddy had done and the result of my disclosure. When the conference ended, I had a promise that further action would be taken.

The following week I sat before the school psychologist taking tests. We never discussed my reason for being there, but she promised that we would talk again in a week or so. At that point, guilt about the "made-up" dream caught up with me. After class the following day, I confessed to my teacher that I had not actually dreamed the episode in my essay. As I lingered, hoping for some kind of understanding or word of forgiveness, three other students walked into the room. Turning from me, the teacher calmly asked them, "What do you think of someone who makes up a story and then allows another person to try to help them on the basis of that lie?"

I had uncovered my wounds to her, and she washed them with acid! All communication came to a halt. Both she and the school psychologist abandoned any evidence of concern. My English grades never rose above a "D" after that. I was hard-pressed to complete any future assignments, and only my previous class work kept me from failing the course.

Then I discovered boys. Acting on that discovery would involve some changes, ones that would not be approved at home. Marge was strict, demanding an accounting for every minute of my day. Makeup was forbidden, and she purchased all of my clothing, often a size larger than I required so that I wouldn't look "sexy." I began to stock a supply of makeup in my locker at school. The scarf or blouse that I wore with a sweater when I left the house in the morning was usually removed before I arrived at the bus stop. Skirts that hung limply from oversized waistbands were pinned and belted until they met my specifications.

While there was no question of "dating," there was nothing to keep me from the cars of boyfriends during lunch and skipped study halls. All I had to do to "stay out of trouble" was remember to wash my face and retie my scarf before I arrived home in the afternoon.

I was allowed to attend chaperoned school functions. Once inside the door, with the proper "stamp" on my hand, I was free to do as I pleased until the time I would be retrieved by one of my parents. Always governed by the fear of discovery, I seldom went far—usually to the parked car of the current boy that I was "dating." But I played a dangerous game.

"Stupid" and "unattractive" by Marge's definitions, I surmised that the key to acceptance and affection lay in my sexuality. Hugging, kissing and petting were the symbols of those elusive prizes; I was determined to get all that I could without surrendering my virginity, and I seemed to possess an uncanny instinct as to the limitations of a boy's endurance. When a relationship became uncomfortably demanding, I broke it. I never made a mistake. As I look back on those years, I stand in awe at the grace of God in my life to protect me from serious physical injury while He waited patiently for me to turn to Him. Brazen as my actions were, this sexual "acting out," so common to many incest victims, bothered my conscience and caused deeper guilt feelings than I had experienced before. It also brought my self-esteem to new lows.

Early in my senior year of high school, Marge announced that I would be allowed to date. The only qualification was that I was not to "bring home any trash." There was little consolation in my liberation. I knew that few of my friends were within the range of Marge's definition of acceptability. On one occasion I did risk a "double date" with another couple. As it was a school night, there was a 10:00 curfew, but that did not deter us from purchasing and drinking several six-packs of beer. It was one of the few times since the eighth grade pajama party that I indulged in any sort of heavy drinking. My anger and frustration had been translated into a rebellion that grew like cancer. The confining attitudes I dealt with at home were like a dam holding that rebellion back, and only the smallest crack in that confinement was sufficient weakness to bring near disaster.

My original assessment of Marge's attitude toward my friends had been correct; Daddy followed us in his car. He saw the beer cans sailing out of the window as we neared home, and he saw my "date" and me kissing in the back seat. They were waiting to confront me when I arrived home. Dating privileges were suspended for the remainder of the year.

In the morning I was kept home from school. Marge took me into the living room for a serious discussion. It was the second and final portion of my formal sex education. They were both upset about the beer, but what was more unsettling to them was the kissing that Daddy had observed. "Sex," Marge informed me, "is why people get married." To me, "sex" was intercourse, not a few casual kisses in a back seat. I could hardly understand why any woman would engage in it willingly outside of the possibility of producing a child. The irony was not lost on me. It was "all right" for Daddy to do what he had done, but not for a boy to give me a few kisses.

Unable even to begin to comprehend the concept that Marge was discussing, I put it aside. Her statement, however, was to have far greater effect on me than either of us would realize for a long time. The following week I resumed my normal standard of duplicity.

My high school career was drawing to a close. "The Future" was a vague concept that I seldom, if ever, probed. A girl could get married at age eighteen, but outside of that, there was no possibility of real independence until twenty-one. Marriage did not seem a probability, so I supposed that I would find a secretarial position and mark time until I was able to move out of the house. Daddy wanted me to go on to school, but I'd had quite my fill of education for the time being, and wouldn't even consider the thought. As graduation neared, he gave up trying to pressure me. One night, as we drove home from my after-school job, he asked, "What do you want for a graduation present?"

The other girls in my class were collecting silverware, crystal and china, none of which held any interest for me. For lack of a better answer, I chose the most improbable thing I could think of. "Oh, I don't know. I guess I'd like a car."

My response had been a stalling tactic. As far as I was concerned, it had been no answer at all. The house we lived in, the two late-model cars driven by my parents, and Daddy's thriving business all attested to the fact that we were "well to do," but I never dreamed that my request would ever fall within the range of serious consideration. His reply confirmed that, and then qualified it. "No, you can't have a car. I would have bought one for you if you were going on to school, but not now."

Several weeks later he ventured to ask again. "I told you what I wanted," I replied. "I can't think of anything else." He kept silent. In truth, I hadn't bothered to give the subject any thought at all. I wondered what he would come up with. It would be interesting to see. He would give me a graduation present, and it would probably be something expensive.

The morning after graduation, a three-year-old coupe in like-new condition stood in our driveway. The title was in my name, and the insurance had been paid for an entire year. Driving instruction had been arranged. I may never fully understand all of the reasons for that car, but it changed my life. I felt as if I had been given wings. Daddy must have been shattered by my response. I was so overwhelmed that my "thank you" was barely audible. I'm truly sorry for that.

Finding a full-time job was the first order of business. Not wishing to spend any more time than necessary around the house, I took the first position offered to me. Unfortunately, the job demanded far more maturity and experience than were at my command. Realizing that I was treading on dangerous ground, I decided to leave of my own volition, before I was fired. I began to investigate the possibilities of going on to school.

Teacher training seemed the only reasonable option. I loved children, and investigation showed that there were several schools, not too distant, which would allow for entry before the year was finished. Daddy was delighted, and so was I—but for different reasons. I would no longer have to live at home.

CHAPTER FIVE

Mike

The mind is its own place, and in itself
Can make a Heaven of Hell, a Hell of Heaven

John Milton
Paradise Lost

Satan's lines concerning heaven and hell in *Paradise Lost* would be most convincing were it not for the fact that less than 100 lines earlier in Milton's classic, we find the Deceiver and his compatriots hastening to remove themselves from the flaming lake. He was right: mind can transcend body—to a point. There are some who even manage to play the game for a lifetime, but not without price. If one will face truth, there must come the admission that there are some things that hurt—and they hurt terribly.

Just as incest doesn't begin "yesterday," it will never end "tomorrow." Even out of the range of daily contact with the abused who had become my abusers, my wounds still bled. More wounds were to come—though they were from a different source they were equally painful, and they served to reinforce all the negative attitudes that I had accumulated concerning myself.

I met Bob soon after high school graduation. Home from college for the summer, he was the kind of boy I had often admired from afar. Clean-cut and popular, he was far beyond my aspirations, but he asked me out. The invitations repeated, and within weeks I had changed my entire image. Clothing, makeup and mannerisms became those of the typical "all-American" girl. Bob's kindness and attention flowered in a happiness I'd never thought possible.

His friends became mine. With a whole group being supportive, my self-image soared. By the time Bob left for school in the fall, I knew that I loved him. Daily, letters crossed in the mail. During the Christmas holidays we were inseparable. New Year's Eve he proposed marriage. I accepted without hesitation.

With my real needs of respect and caring met, there had been no need for me to "push" for the kind of physical contact I had so sought after in high school. Bob and I had really been quite circumspect. Suddenly, he began to be more demanding. "No," became increasingly frequent in my vocabulary when we were alone together. I tried to talk to him about it. Sex frightened me. I needed time and understanding in the context of a trusting relationship, and the desire to remain a virgin until our wedding night was strong. Bob's only reply to the expression of that desire was, "We'll see." He continued to pressure; I continued to resist. By March the engagement had ended. Bob's friends drifted away, and I was again alone. Convinced once more that my only desirability lay in sexuality, my self-image plummeted. There was no heaven in this hell; the pain was very real.

Life was put on hold. All the motions were there: I finished my second term at college, searched for and found a summer job, and even did some casual dating, but none of it seemed real. I couldn't afford reality; it held too much unpleasantness.

During the summer I was introduced to Mike. He was different; older than most of the fellows that I had dated, he possessed a maturity that was comforting. One date led to another, the second to a third, and soon we were seeing each other socially several times a week. In contrast to their attitude towards Bob, my parents disliked Mike almost on sight. Six weeks after we met, he offered a diamond for the ring finger of my left hand. I accepted, and the pain of Bob's rejection was bandaged.

We kept the engagement semi-secret at first. With the regulations Marge and Daddy imposed (I still had a 12:00 curfew on weekends), and their initial dislike of Mike, I could hardly imagine that they would accept the idea of engagement so soon. When we announced our intentions some six weeks later, the objections were vehement. Insisting that Mike had no financial future, neither of them would even look at the ring I wore so proudly. I was of age, however, and they were helpless to oppose the decision I had made. They were rapidly losing control over my life.

I usually came home from school for the weekend, arriving late Friday night. By concentrating on homework, laundry and necessary shopping, I cleared away most of my responsibilities by Saturday evening. Mike and I would find a quiet restaurant that didn't object to our lingering over several cups of coffee for conversation. We took long drives and even longer walks, and we painted a future that seemed breathtakingly wonderful, if idealistic. On Sundays I would attend the earliest church service with Daddy, teach a Sunday school class immediately following, and then drive with Mike to his parents' home about thirty miles south.

Late that fall as I came into the driveway one morning after Sunday school, Daddy burst from the house and accused me, in one breath, of coming in at 3 A.M. and being drunk. Forbidding me to leave with Mike for the afternoon, he got into his car, promising to continue the discussion when he returned. I was stunned. The accusations were false, and neither my actions of the night before nor my contact with him earlier at church had prepared me for such an outburst.

By the time I reached the room that I shared with Grandma my face was stained with outraged tears. Grandma's day had arrived. "Do you love him?" She had never before been so tender, not even with me.

I nodded.

"Then decide what it is you want from life and take it. If you give up now you'll never be free." Her last sentence convinced me. She realized, far better than I, what the consequences of the next few minutes would be.

Grandma walked with me to answer the door, listened while I explained my tear-stained face to Mike, smiled at his declaration of protection, and gently but firmly pushed us out of the door, closing it behind us.

When we returned that evening, Marge and Daddy banished Mike from the house. They had an ultimatum for me: either leave with Mike now and never come back, or tell him good-bye and break the engagement immediately. There was only one question on my lips as I sped toward Mike's waiting car: "Are you willing to take me with you, now?" He was. I packed my suitcase and left. The choice had not been difficult. They had offered me the thing I wanted most, final freedom from their control. There was no possibility of my considering whether or not this was the road I wanted to follow. As far as I was concerned, it was the only road there was. The only consequence I could envision was that I would never have to spend another night under Daddy's roof. Like so many victims of incest, my primary goal was to leave the scene of my pain.

There was also no question of my returning to school. Doing so would only leave me vulnerable to pressure to reverse my decision. Mike took me to his parents' home. They were not surprised to see us, and they were only too happy to provide bed and board for as long as it was required.

Mike returned to his job as a sales trainee, and after a week of emotional readjustment, I found a secretarial position. We began to plan for a February wedding. Now that school was out of the picture, there was no point in waiting.

The relationship between Mike and myself changed drastically. Long conversations of earlier dating months degenerated to a series of brief remarks during television commercials. I scoured the local library, never having found any attraction to the electronic device. Any attempts to interest Mike in reading were futile. Conversation lagged even more. Only after his parents and brothers had gone upstairs to bed would Mike's interest turn to me. Alone, comfortable, secure, it was easy to become increasingly intimate. Marge's remark, "Sex is why people get married," echoed through my head and the concept of sex for pleasure which had once seemed so alien to me was now very understandable.

By mid-January Mike was restless and irritable. Something was wrong. "Too many unpaid bills to take on the financial obligations of marriage," was his reply to my query. I would not force him; I agreed to a postponement. May arrived, and there was still no talk of a ceremony. I would not bring the subject into our conversation. It had to come from him.

Early in June he announced that he would be away for the weekend, as he had a short training assignment in another town. There was an automobile accident involving Mike. His parents broke the news that he had been hospitalized.

We drove to see him. His broken leg was a matter for

concern, but it didn't explain the strange signals that were flashing back and forth between Mike and his mother. The car had been totally destroyed, and a woman's life was in serious jeopardy. I chose to attribute the subtle interaction between mother and son to the gravity of the situation.

About a week after Mike was released from the hospital he took me aside for a "talk." My parents wanted to see me, and Mike knew the subject of their concern. He decided that my enlightenment should come from him. I heard, for the first time, of the one fact about the accident that I had missed; it was the newspaper account that he and his parents had contrived for me not to see. There was a married woman in the car with him at the time of the accident. His explanation of why he was on a side road with her at midnight, "making a wrong turn taking her home after work," was difficult to understand, as was his reason for hiding her presence from me, but I chose to believe him. I was too afraid not to. He lost his job because of the circumstances of that accident. My parents never made the desired contact.

Storm clouds were gathering which I could not totally ignore, but they were less frightening than a future that offered an admission that I had believed in a lie. Had I known the information which revealed itself nine months later, my actions might have been different. The woman who had been with Mike gave birth to a child, and the most significant factor in that event was that she felt it necessary to inform him.

Mike's leg healed and he found another job. He would be transferred to another town, and I knew that if we were not married when he left, we never would be. I waited and, lacking any proposals for action, proceeded to make plans that would take me from his parents' home.

Suddenly Mike realized that I wasn't just playing games. I really intended to leave, and he knew I would do so as soon as it was practical. He was ready to talk. With a calmness that surprised even me, I explained my fears and dissatisfaction with his unwillingness to make a permanent commitment. As I did so, I removed the engagement ring and placed it between us, offering Mike his freedom. I was fully prepared for any decision he would make. Three weeks later we were married.

Our wedding day was difficult beyond description. Amid growing reservations, I made vows that I was uncertain of being able to keep. At one point in the ceremony I actually considered turning and walking out of the church, but I didn't, and so became part of statistics yet to be established: the marriages of incest victims tend to be troubled marriages, and the abused very often marry abusers. That second feature of our marriage would not become overtly apparent for years.

We were transferred south. Mike traveled five days a week and adjustment was difficult in a town where I knew no one except the people I worked with. With Mike home only on weekends, our adjustment to each other was in a constant state of fluctuation. Desperately lonely, I begged for a child. He insisted that we were not financially able to consider a baby, but brought home grandiose dreams of new cars, boats, and expensive camera equipment. The confusion and frustration were more than I could tolerate. Three years after our marriage, the divorce I was considering was halted only when he lost his job. We moved back to his hometown.

I reasoned that with Mike home every night we at least stood a chance to build a life together. I didn't count on the television set. All discussions were postponed until the cowboys, detectives and Johnny Carson had been retired for the night. My discontent could then be silenced by our physical relationship. The child that

I so longed for was no closer to becoming a reality than it had been the week we were married. I left. Mike found me at the home of a friend, and again, in the face of my drastic action, he was willing to talk.

Davey was born about a year later. Reflecting much of my own insecurity and nervousness, he was colicky and difficult during the first few months. Some of the changes in Mike, however, had been real and permanent, and he proved to be a genuine help and a good father. At last we had a common interest—Davey. There was, unfortunately, no agreement on my desire for a second child.

The disagreement was minor. Convinced that time would change Mike's mind, the next few years were undeniably happy. Then changes began to take place, subtle, at first. *Playboy* magazines appeared in the living room each month. Sex between Mike and me had never been much of a problem, and although there were some things that I could barely tolerate because of my incest experience, I never placed any limitations on our activity. When I didn't respond to the magazines, however, I began to hear stories from Mike, stories about friends who were seeking their pleasure elsewhere because their wives wouldn't cooperate.

I began to "cooperate" with his new ideas. "Cooperation" in our sexual terminology soon had companion words like "innovation" and "initiative" and "unique." I became innovative and initiating and unique. I also began to dread sex. Unless it was "new," according to Mike, it was "out." But there was really nothing new, only increasing depths of degradation to which I had to submit. With Davey to consider, I no longer felt free to leave, nor could I psychologically consider any course of action which might give Mike the least cause for infidelity. I was trapped in a new nightmare.

Early mornings often found me sitting alone in an

unlighted living room, smoking cigarette after cigarette, wondering what to do. After several weeks of these midnight sessions, I began to ask myself, "What am I here for, anyway?" As merely a sex partner for Mike and mother to Davey, my death would bring a few tears, a few weeks of sadness, and I would be replaced—as easily as one replaces a piece of furniture or an automobile. Surely, life had to have more significance than what I was experiencing. If it didn't, I would end it.

I started to read my Bible. Going back to first causes, I reasoned that if there was a God then there was a reason for my life. Religion had never helped me before; there were thousands of religions, each saying a different thing. If God had revealed Himself, I would find Him in the Bible. What people had to say about the subject was no longer relevant.

Beginning with Genesis I continued, sometimes doggedly, through 2 Kings. My personal guilt increased to almost unbearable limits. There was much that I didn't understand, but what I did understand was that I was personally unacceptable in the eyes of a holy God. What other people had done really didn't matter; what I had done would condemn me for eternity. I decided to try the New Testament. Midnight sessions were no longer enough. Every spare moment that I could find was spent drinking in the words, as a man coming from the desert drinks in water. Again, much of what I read I didn't understand, but I did see that in Jesus Christ I had found a person who loved me apart from my sexuality, who was willing to hear me when I had a problem, and was willing to die to prove His love genuine. All I had to do was figure out how to make it a part of my life.

During several more midnight sessions, I no longer just thought about my problems—I prayed. Still, something was missing. Finally, climbing back into bed about 3 A.M. one morning, the tears of frustration overwhelmed me. With Mike sleeping and unaware that I had ever left our bedroom, I prayed, "God, I know you're out there somewhere, but you're too far away for me to reach. Please, will you reach out for me and make yourself known to me?"

My request was answered immediately. Flooded with a peace that I had never known existed I said, "Thank you," and fell asleep with a smile on my face.

CHAPTER SIX

The Road
to Forgiveness

> *This is certain, that a man that studieth revenge keeps his own wounds green, which otherwise would heal and do well.*
>
> Francis Bacon

The problems that Mike and I were having were not cleared up in a miraculous overnight working of God. They got worse. His newly-established insurance agency was a dramatic success. Each new achievement brought with it a new tension and, for some reason, a new necessity to prove his power through new sexual experimentation. I began to have nightmares; each one a variation on the same theme—Mike forcing me to have sex with my stepfather. I would wake drenched with icy perspiration. The abuse of my marriage was becoming confused with the incest of my childhood, and I seemed as helpless to deal with the one as I had been with the other. At the same time, however, I was fully aware of a new strength supporting me. Not only was God willing to listen, He believed me, and, when the time was right, He would provide a solution.

Mike became openly antagonistic toward me. Religion had always frightened him. Even when we attended weddings and funerals, he made sure that he would enter the church at the last possible moment, and he would be the first one to leave the building, even to the point of rudeness. At the same time that he was berating my new faith, however, he admitted that some very positive changes were taking place. Assured of the forgiveness of my sins, and secure in the love of my Savior, I no longer needed to vent my anger and frustration in tears and verbal tirades. My smoking habit, well-established at more than two packs a day after twenty years, dropped away. It simply did not seem consistent with an indwelling Christ. Tension lines began to disappear from my face.

On one occasion, and one occasion only, Mike allowed me to share with him the reasons for those changes. Despite the evidence, he dismissed the testimony of my life and the authority of the Bible as a "bunch of fairy tales" that I would outgrow in a year or so, and adopted a course of action apparently designed to speed that end as well as soothe his own fears. His casual drinking became more serious. The "cocktail before dinner" became two, then three. His language became increasingly foul. His effort to demoralize me both emotionally and sexually led me to wonder what the outcome would be.

About a year after my conversion, my stepfather had a stroke. It was serious, and in view of the life-threatening nature of his illness, I found that I was increasingly bothered by scriptural injunctions to forgive those who have wronged us. I was, however, unable to come to terms with the pain and anger that the very sight of him evoked: twenty years of hatred is not dissolved overnight. An attitude of detached friendliness remained where I knew there should be warm concern, but it was all that I could manage. I would need to see him in a new light before I could even begin to forgive, and that would take drastic changes in my life.

Two weeks after Daddy's release from the hospital Mike suffered a heart attack. He did not survive.

The funeral parlor was crowded. Encouragements, loving arms, offers of assistance in managing the affairs of the immediate weeks and months ahead were all a comfort to me. The tribulations of our marriage were temporarily forgotten, and I saw in the casket only the tender lover of our earlier years together. My grief was very real.

During a brief time when few people were present, I turned from the casket to rest in a nearby chair. As I did so, my stepfather came into the range of my view. Still pale and drawn from his own physical ordeal, he dropped his head into his hands and wept. For one moment I knew that his pain and mine were the same. Despite all the differences, he identified with my loss. A new emotion swept through me, forever nameless, akin to both understanding and pity. That night as I waited for sleep to come, I mentioned Daddy in my prayers for the first time in my life. "Father, I don't know if I can ever forgive him for what he's done to me, but you can. Whatever else he has done, please, don't hold *this* sin against his charge. And, Lord, work what you will in my heart if you mean for me to forgive him."

Daddy never recovered his full strength. With Mike's death, the conflict between my parents and me eased somewhat and I began to spend more time with them. The more I saw Daddy, the more I realized that his weakness was not all of his body. A prisoner of guilt and sin, he was chained to the habits that would help him to live with his past. Drinking heavily and smoking several packs of cigarettes a day, he was allowing his life to drain away by inches. His foul language and violent temper were only devices to mask his insecurity, pain and fear. Unable to face life, he was even less prepared to face death.

Nonetheless, I could not speak. Years of alienation had made it virtually impossible for me to discuss anything more important with him than last week's weather.

A job opportunity about six months later made it seem wise to move to another Midwest location. Eight-year-old Davey and I left town. Our new lives had begun. We kept in touch with my stepparents by phone and annual visits, and the conviction to forgive gnawed at my soul like a canker.

The nightmares went away, but the conviction didn't. Every time I read one of those innumerable (and far-too-transparent-for-comfort) passages about forgiveness, my guilt would come rushing back like a tidal wave. The thing that God was commanding me to do was the thing that was not within me. The hurt was too deep. The news that Daddy was in the hospital brought new impetus to the conflict about a year after Davey and I had moved. I argued with God.

"Lord, how can I ever forgive him for what he did to me?"

"What is the difference between what he did to you and all of his other sins?"

"Nothing, really, except that I was the victim." I found myself getting uncomfortable.

"What particular sin of his will condemn him to hell?"

"Only the sin of not accepting Jesus Christ as his personal Savior."

"Not his violation of your body?"

"No, not even that." My answers were less bold. The focus of my hatred was becoming blurred.

"What then, is the difference between his sin and yours?"

"None—except that mine has been forgiven through the blood of Christ."

"If I can forgive you, why are you unable to forgive your stepfather?"

"But Lord, what he did to me was so terrible!" My throat constricted with tears as I clung to the last vestiges of self.

"What did your sins do to my Son?"

"They nailed Him to a cross."

I sat silently for a long time after that. There was no question now: I would, by choice of will, forgive.

Dear Daddy,

This letter is long overdue. Annie called to tell me that you are in the hospital again, and I can't rest until I've said what's on my mind. There are so many things we can never discuss, even in a letter, and many more that we can never talk about face to face. That's just the way things are. I can write some of those things, however. You will understand.

First of all, I want to thank you. There are so many things that could have been different. You could have said "no" when Uncle John offered Annie and me up for adoption, and I guess if you had insisted, Annie and I could have been separated, too. I'm so grateful that neither of those things happened.

I want to thank you, too, for some of the values that you tried to instill in me. I know that you meant well, even though I was rebellious. The lessons about economy and "putting something away" and the importance of continuing my education were not lost entirely. I know them now.

The real reason I'm writing is to share my thanks in a way that is very special to me. You know about the changes in my life about the time that Mike died. Those changes were due to a Person who is so important to me that I would die before I would deny Him, and I want to share Him with you.

I've watched you for a long time as you've gone to church and given extra money to help the pastor or some cause that you thought needed your support. And I've watched as you've joined organizations and put in a lot of time and hard work to further the good things that they do, but we need more than good things in our lives. What we need is a Person, a relationship with Christ. It's not what we do, or what we know that provides the way to heaven and eternal life, it's Who we know, and that important "Who" is Jesus.

The way we get to know Him is to acknowledge before God that it was Christ's death on the cross which paid for our sins, not anything which we ourselves have done. We can't "buy a ticket" at any price, and we can't "sneak in" through the back gate. He will give it, free for the asking, if we will just acknowledge Him, and stop depending on ourselves.

There's so much more that still can't be said this way. I've asked Pastor Allen to come to visit you. That way you can ask questions. Please, listen to what he has to say. It's important. I'd like to know that we will spend eternity together, with God.

I love you,
Katie

Despite the letter and the pastor's visit, Daddy still did not understand the plan of salvation, but he did understand that I had forgiven him. There could be no mention of incest (it would be years before I would make an association between that term and what had happened between us); his illness and our total relationship prevented any recollection of the experience in actual words, but my meaning was clear to both of us.

He cried when he held me the next time I came home, and I didn't cringe when he touched me. It was the beginning of a new relationship for us, one that began when I wrote the words, "I love you."

For the first time in my life, weeks and months went by without the horror coming back to mind, but still it would not go away completely. I felt a reluctance and resentment about "home" that I didn't understand. I prayed, claiming the promise of James, "If any of you lacks wisdom, he should ask God, who gives generously to all without finding fault, and it will be given to him" (1:5).

The next day Marge phoned, and before our conversation was ended I knew that my problem was with her. Her lack of understanding, her refusal to believe me, her emotional abandonment when I needed her the most had hurt as much as, if not more than, all of the indignities that had gone before. She knew—she had to—yet she denied my disclosure to protect her own security.

Suddenly I understood. The more I examined the patterns of Marge's life, the more I realized her insecurity. My accusation had threatened everything that was important to her: financial security, the security of her marriage, and the security of a faultless reputation. Emotionally, she was unable to face any evidence that threatened her so much. No wonder, then, that when a doctor held out a thread of hope that my accusation was the product of a teenage imagination, Marge grasped it and used it as a lifeline to secure her world.

Her domineering personality may not have been the typical one for mothers in incestuous families, but her insecurities and denial systems were, and they had been operating at full capacity. Any hope of dealing openly with issues was flickering and unrealistic, at least for the time being.

My animosity dissolved rapidly in the face of the new understandings, and forgiveness came more easily. We, too, began building a new relationship, one based on my realization of her needs.

One more area for resolution remained, and that was perhaps the most painful resolution of them all. I had to face the problem of my relationship with Mike.

Had I been wise, the marriage would never have taken place, but victims of incest are usually not wise; they are vulnerable, and they are often seeking a way out of their dilemma. Mike had been my way out, and for that I needed his forgiveness as much as I needed to forgive him for turning our most private moments into degrading orgies. We had both been unable to distinguish love from sex, and our relationship moldered in the bedroom. Unexposed to the sunlight of communication and genuine caring, our marriage began to die before we ever realized the possibilities for its life.

Mike was gone. I could not ask for his forgiveness, nor could I tell him of mine for him. I did the next best thing and opened my heart before the Lord. He, and He alone is the decider of life and death, and to quarrel with His decision to end the marriage when He did is pointless. David is a happy reminder of all that was good about those years. He is grown now, and I see in him many of Mike's good qualities. They would have liked each other.

The pattern of incest and abuse is broken. It has not been passed through me to my son. As a teenager, David's idea of abuse was not being able to use the car on Saturday night. In order to keep him from hard feelings toward those he should love, I have asked him not to read this book until he is much older, and he assures me that he will not. His concerns lie in building a future for himself, not in digging up the past.

Forgiveness is important. One needs to spend very

little time in the Scriptures to realize that it is one of God's top priorities, and He has not excluded incest. The burden that hatred leaves behind is too heavy to bear. It weighs down the soul to which it is bound and turns the one wronged into a double victim: first, of the wrong committed, and second, of the burden of maintaining the remembrance of pain. Forgiveness loosens those bonds so that the soul is free to soar and be nearer to the God for whom it was created.

I willed forgiveness to each of those involved in my story; from natural parents unable to cope, to a sister who played nasty games; from the leering exhibitionist in the back alley to the rejecting fiancé, and to others who have not been mentioned in these pages.

If "the opera isn't over till the fat lady sings," then for many incest victims, the good lady seems to have disappeared forever sometime during the last intermission. For others, the refrains of the final aria echo sweetly in their ears. The battles have all been fought, the villain has been dealt with on one level or another, and the story has been fully disclosed and resolved. Whether or not we liked it, the opera is over; catharsis has taken place, and we can go home and get on with our lives.

Such was the effect, for me, of writing the original edition of this book. Life moved on to some graduate work, I fell in love with a new career, and I adjusted to the fact that my son was now an adult who not only lived away from home, but in another state. What I didn't realize was that more was to come. This opera had another scene which offered not only further understanding, but resolution beyond anything I could have dreamed.

My Aunt Molly had always been special to me, but the bond between us strengthened. Separated in age by only thirteen years, we are often more like friends or sisters than aunt and niece. Several weeks before the first volume of this book came from the press, we were talking on the phone. Referring to some work that I had published earlier, she asked, "Have you written anything else—I mean, anything that has been published?"

Suddenly, I felt I could trust her. Certainly, neither Marge nor Annie would be able to handle the things contained in the manuscript, but Molly could, if she were told in the right way. Tentatively I told her of my impending "new release," explaining very little and asking her to keep the news to herself for the time being. I would explain when I saw her on my next trip "home."

While I enjoyed a hot cup of tea in her kitchen a few weeks later, Molly bubbled with the multiple enthusiasm of friend, fellow writer and proud aunt. Finally, I interrupted her stream of praise. "I think you need to know what the book is about." She already knew it concerned family, but quietly turned to look at me. "It's about incest," I said.

Even the clock seemed to stop ticking.

"Al?"

I nodded. Another long pause.

"Me, too." Her voice was a whisper. I was the first person she ever told.

We talked for hours. With her, he had been more brazen and less successful. Exhibitionism is disgusting, and finding a man next to you in bed is terrifying, but not life-destroying, especially if you have a relatively healthy self-image—and if your teenaged girlfriend happens to be sharing that same bed with you. Not a "father figure" to her, Al was quickly evicted, and Molly briefly discussed the incident with her friend. They both assumed that "men are just 'that way.'" As far as I know, they both still carry that assumption.

I was sorry for Molly, of course, but the stronger

emotion was relief. She believed me! She had shared in some of my pain! She understood, at least partially, what I had been through. The bonds of our friendship have grown considerably stronger since then. We seldom discuss Al because we share too many other interests.

About two years later, Al died. His health had varied between poor and desperate for several years, and visits home had become more frequent with the knowledge that each could be the last time to see Al alive. Clearly, in his final years, I became the favored daughter for reasons that were known only to us. The letter I had written to him had made a profound difference. After the funeral, I found it in his personal belongings.

His illness had been long and difficult, his mind had been clouded, and caring for him had nearly destroyed Marge's health. For these reasons I was relieved that it was over. Where he spends eternity is between him and God—it has nothing to do with the relationship he had with me. But one thing remained unfinished: the thing I could never say to him while he was alive.

The funeral was small and private with fewer than twenty people in attendance. At one point I found myself alone with the casketed body. As I stared at his frail remains I was nearly overwhelmed with pity for this man who never really knew happiness or fulfillment or himself, and very little of the true meaning of love. Nearly eighty years of life had never yielded their meaning for him. Certainly he could never be adequate to meet the emotional needs of his children; he had never been adequate to meet even his own. I could finally say the words aloud. "Al, I forgive you. I forgive your manipulation of my life, I forgive the pain you caused, I forgive you for never being the father that I needed. I forgive you for using me sexually."

Tears started to flow, and I was fortunate to be able to leave the room before they became a torrent. My sobbing took place in private, and when it was over I was free in a new way. How I wish that Al could have heard those words—all theology aside, perhaps he did.

The third event took place more than a year later, and was unexpected. Sunday morning I was getting ready for church. The next day my yearly visit with Marge would end, and I would go back to my teaching job. Finding that I had completed my routine a little earlier than necessary, I sat down to talk with Marge at the breakfast table. The weekend had been relaxed and easy, and she began to tell me a story about one of her friends. She meant it to be funny, but it involved the humiliation of an emotionally disturbed person, and I found it difficult to laugh.

"I'm sorry," I told her. "I guess I just don't think that's funny."

The world exploded in a blaze of anger as Marge enumerated what she considered my personal deficiencies. Stunned, and totally off guard, I flared back with a general listing of her shortcomings as a parent. The exchanges continued until I stormed out of the room and began to pack my suitcase. After a few minutes, Marge appeared at the door. "I think we should talk," she said rather quietly. My heart stopped; nothing could have prepared me for such an advance in our relationship. I agreed.

Our conversation had a rather rough beginning, but she again surprised me when she said, "I'd like to know what it is that divides us. It always seems like there's something I don't understand."

I trembled and decided that this could well be my last chance to clear the air. "Well, we have the fact that I was the baggage for Annie. I always knew that you didn't really want me."

"I know you feel that way." She didn't deny it. I

didn't press the information that John had confirmed the overheard discussion.

"Then there was the way I was handed around like a bag of groceries, without anyone ever asking what I thought or bothering to tell me what was going on."

"What can you tell a five-year-old?" It seemed better not to mention that no one had even tried. We were too close to the heart of this discussion.

"And then I had my father climbing into my bed." Now Marge was trembling

"Once." She pointed a shaking finger at me.

"No. Eighteen months."

She was quiet for a long time. "That's awful," she said. "Awful." Her shoulders sagged and she stared out of the window. "What did he do?"

The rest of that conversation is indelibly impressed in my memory. I spoke in generalities, giving her only enough information to make the picture real, but she understood. She accepted what I told her, putting her denial system on hold, and she helped me to understand what had happened "behind the scenes" on that awful day thirty years before. Al convinced her that he had made a "single pass" at me. She had accepted his explanation—at the time she could admit to no other.

Her one attempt to bleach the affair came when she saw the photograph of Al holding me indecently. "Why didn't you take his hand away?" I showed her my fingers straining to do just that. She said no more.

Monday morning I lingered. We needed the time. When I finally walked out of the door, she said, "I hope you've got it out of your system. I'm not sure I'll ever get it out of mine."

Marge is still Marge. She "forgets" what she knows and still eagerly points out the shortcomings of others. When she discovered the story of Sonia's abuse by her paternal grandfather, she enthusiastically shared the news of his downfall. Only a gentle reminder was necessary to subdue her zeal. But, her attitude has changed. Our relationship has altered permanently and positively. She is more willing to allow me to be who I am. I, in turn, try to be more tolerant of her "opinions." They no longer threaten me.

Confrontation is not a necessity in order to be a "survivor"—to achieve a fulfilled and happy life, but it adds a dimension of release that is nearly impossible to describe. Not all attempts are as successful as mine, but where any chance exists to "settle the matter," it is more than worth the pain it temporarily causes.

The opera is over. The lady has sung her song. My life will go on with the same kinds of problems and joys that other people experience. I only hope that I will be able to help others who are waiting for the curtain calls of their "operas" to better understand what has happened to them and how they, too, can get on with their lives.

CHAPTER SEVEN

Annie's Children

There is ruin and decay
   In the House on the Hill:
They are all gone away
There is nothing more to say.

E. A. Robinson

For twenty-five years I thought that my victimization was unique, if not within the society in which we live, then at least within the confines of my own family. I was mistaken. But to understand what happened to Annie and her children we need to go back to the time when we were young.

My happiest times were in the grassy fields. I captured fireflies and butterflies, grasshoppers and toads, green snakes and turtles. Anything that had life held an absolute fascination for me, as long as it didn't threaten to sink teeth or stinger into my skin. Whatever my emotional state of being, I glowed with physical good health and a love of nature.

Annie, in contrast, was occupied with colds and ear infections, measles and mumps, bronchial pneumonia and tonsillitis. About the time Marge threw away the batch of medications for one illness, another would show itself. If Annie got too cold, she got sick. If Annie got too excited, she got sick. If Annie got too upset, she got sick. If we got into a playful mood, there would be Marge hovering over us: "Stop that! Annie will get sick." For a number of years my younger sister was the "fourth person" to join us at the dinner table—when she wasn't confined to her bed. Fortunately, her health improved somewhat with age.

By the time that she turned twelve, things started to fit back together for us. She was becoming interested in boys and clothes and makeup, and I had won enough victories in each area so that my experience was of interest to her. Perhaps because our stepparents served as a target for my hatred and anger, perhaps because I longed to recapture the old relationship we had shared, perhaps because I just wanted someone to be close, I welcomed her with open arms. We were "sisters" again, and I carried no grudges. But I worried. "Will he try the same thing with her?" "Should I warn her?" The last summer that I lived at home, I watched, but I really didn't spend enough time with the two of them together to make any valid observations. Daddy was gone a lot, and even my concern for Annie was not motivation enough for me to spend an evening at home when I could be elsewhere.

She was the "treasure child," I decided. Daddy and Marge loved her. It was for her that the adoption had taken place. If I tried to warn her I could very well spoil what had always seemed sweet and good. Besides, although I loved her, I really couldn't trust her not to betray a confidence. I opted for silence. She seemed secure. She was not, but it was better that I didn't know. It would have changed nothing.

Years later, when the two of us finally were able to at least talk around the fringes of the subject—the one brief glimpse that she gave me into the beginnings of her turmoil—she revealed that all he had ever really done to her was to fondle her breasts. At the time of that revelation I was relieved that she had to endure only so small a thing. What I did not realize was that the trauma is not always in direct proportion to the severity of the sexual abuse. Once the father-daughter relationship is altered, many factors can affect the eventual outcome. As my sister, she was subject to many of the same family disturbances that I had known. There is, at present, no practical way of determining how cognizant she is of my incest experience. What she may have seen could have done immeasurable damage.

Knowing that I had been part of the "baggage" that came with Annie, violation was traumatic for me, but I dealt with that trauma with the same determination for survival that had developed through all of my other conflicts—and I had Grandma. Annie was different. Not only was she fragile and unprotected emotionally, unschooled to deal with any emotional crisis, but she and my grandmother were openly antagonistic toward each other. Annie had no one to accept her as she was. Once I left home, she had no emotional support whatsoever within the family. She nurtured her resentments privately and went on to a more violent rebellion than I had ever dared.

Annie discovered her powers early, and used them to suit her pleasure. Whenever she was threatened by a denial of her wishes, her fragile health could be counted on to reverse the decision. Dating, smoking openly before my stepparents, and purchasing the clothing of her choice were privileges gained early. On the day that Mike and I were married I saw the effects of that lack of discipline and how it would color her future relationships with the opposite sex.

Arriving just moments before the ceremony, fifteen-year-old Annie and my stepparents sat near the rear of the church. Although Daddy and Marge had announced their intention to leave immediately after the ceremony, they agreed to leave Annie behind, to be brought home later by Uncle John and his wife. The church reception was to be followed, according to local custom, by a more intimate gathering at my in-laws' home.

During the rather busy afternoon I lost track of my sister, but as evening approached and Mike and I were preparing to leave, she came hurriedly into the living room where I stood and asked if she could speak to me alone. Her sense of urgency compelled me to hurry with her up the stairs to my room. Dramatically throwing herself across the bed she declared, "Oh, Katie, what am I going to do?"

My heart began to sink. She had spent the afternoon with Mike's younger brother. Tom was very mature for his age, and knowing the attitudes and practices of the crowd that he kept company with did nothing to reassure me that the hours spent "in the field" had been entirely innocent. Annie's obvious distress had me thinking the worst. She confided that she was "in love."

Some indirect questioning revealed that the necking and petting had at least stayed above the waist and that all clothing had remained intact. Dismayed and relieved at the same time, I reluctantly agreed to assist the couple in corresponding. Our stepparents' attitude over my marriage would necessitate a secretive correspondence, but time, distance, and the age of the two involved, I reasoned, would soon cool their interest. I was correct. Three months later she was "in love" with someone considerably more tangible than the brother of her brother-in-law with whom she could only correspond. Within a year she was "in love" with Dan. Football hero, good-looking and even more insecure than she was, he pursued her unwaveringly. Eighteen months after their meeting she was carrying his child—they were unmarried.

It could all be dismissed as emotional immaturity,

except for the fact that since her divorce she has continued with identical behavior patterns. In one six-month period of time she was counted to be "in love" no less than five times, often making her declaration shortly after her first date with a man. Her search for security and acceptance continues, desperate and unrewarding.

Annie and Dan were finally married when her pregnancy had progressed to six months. Mike and I served as witnesses to the brief ceremony before a civil judge. As we drove home, Dan asked, "Now, how long do I have before I can divorce her without paying alimony?" Annie made no comment as Mike informed his new brother-in-law that it was already too late. Years later, when the divorce was final, I asked Annie why she had allowed the abuse that Dan heaped upon her. The answer was heartbreaking:

"I didn't think I deserved any better. Besides, once I had sex with him, I thought I was married to him in the eyes of God anyway. You have to get legally married before you can be legally divorced."

Low self-image, insecurity, rebellion, and confusion had brought Annie to the arms of a man who would abuse her both physically and emotionally for the next seventeen years. She had made her "escape" from home, but she paid a terrible price. I saw bruises on her body before the baby was born. She had been receiving them before it was conceived.

Had Annie and Dan any opportunity to attain a measure of independence, the problem might have resolved itself more quickly, either in arriving at workable solutions or ending in early divorce. As it was, they had Marge to deal with.

Mary De Young, in discussing the dynamics of incestuous families, states:

Like incest victims themselves, the mothers are rendered insecure and extremely dependent as a result of these experiences. They are also infused with a large dose of separation anxiety that is likely to be pervasive throughout their adult lives.[1]

Later in the same discussion she states that the mothers often become "passive and detached."[2] It took years for me to realize Marge's insecurities, but "passive" and "detached" were never adjectives which could be applied with even the remotest degree of accuracy. Unable to effectively cope with her own marriage, a cauldron of fiery tempers, resistance and self-will, she seemed determined to manage the lives of others. Always in the guise of "helping" or "family responsibility" or "because of the babies," she directed and controlled and assisted until her victims either capitulated or fled in self-defense. Annie was no exception.

Three months after the wedding, Sonia was born. A year later Nora made her entrance into Annie's family. Twice within the first five years Annie sought means to end the beatings and drunken tirades that Dan inflicted upon her. Each time she filed for legal separation, however, Marge and Daddy took Dan aside for "a nice little talk," promised some new financial assistance to ease the tension, and walked away smiling, convinced that the marriage would now succeed.

Dan's job as a truck driver paid well, but intervention by Marge and Daddy was so effective that it was nearly ten years before he ever paid for a single piece of furniture in his own house. During that same time, Marge bought and paid for all of the clothing worn by Sonia and Nora. Annie's high medical bills were often forwarded to Daddy. Whenever Marge did not approve of Annie's method of child rearing (which was often), she threatened either to remove financial support or to

83

gain custody of the two girls. Annie's life was one of total frustration.

Dan was an alcoholic. It was not unusual for 20% or more of the weekly budget to be directed toward the local bar. As our stepparents increased their control over Annie's family, Dan's insecurities increased, and so did his drinking. Parental support came to an abrupt end when discovery was made of the amount involved. Annie decided that it was time to find work. Her home situation changed dramatically.

Sonia, the older daughter, assumed responsibility for nearly all of the household tasks. By the time she was eleven she cleaned, cooked, and managed the household. She and Annie argued violently over her authoritarian attitudes, which she also asserted over her younger sister. Before long, when Dan came home drunk, she accepted, along with her other duties, the "responsibility" of taking him into her bed. Dan, seriously abused as a child both physically and emotionally, became an abuser not only of his wife, but of his own children.

Boldly boasting that she was the one who "ran the house," Sonia carefully guarded her relationship with her father. At age fifteen, she found her paternal grandfather beginning to pay special attention to her. Before long she found that she was as unable to refuse her grandfather's advances as she had those of her father.

Sonia married when she was eighteen. Within a year she bore bruises that indicated possible abuse by her husband. He travels a good deal, and "overnight" guests are often reported furtively seeking to reach their cars, parked a block or two away, without being noticed. Emotionally she remains closely tied to both her father and her grandfather and violently defends them against criticism of any kind. Anorectic, alcoholic, and a chain smoker, her hands visibly tremble when she uses them. Her driver's license has been revoked because of drunk driving. Divorce has been considered by both Sonia and her husband—and Sonia has not yet celebrated her twenty-first birthday.

While one would hesitate to attribute all of these effects solely to the incest itself, many of them are common to incest victims. They almost certainly stem from a common psychology. In Sonia's case, it could well be a life-threatening psychology.

When the younger daughter, Nora, repelled the advances of her father, he contented himself with producing bruises conveniently located where they would be covered by her clothing. Annie said nothing. Only after repeated attempts to run away did Nora finally confide that Annie, too, had lashed out and performed her share of abuse.

No conclusive statistics for incest demonstrate the incidence of the abused becoming the abusers, but Annie and her family were not statistics. They were living, breathing, hurting people—and there was nowhere for them to turn for help.

As a sibling, rather than the actual victim of sexual abuse, it seemed for a time that Nora had faced the events of her past, dealt with them, and put them behind her. Shortly after the birth of her second child, her apparent resolution disintegrated. In a series of infidelities, combined with serious child neglect, she effectively destroyed her own marriage. History demonstrates that such instabilities are not uncommon in a situation such as Nora's.[3] Unless she is helped, she will most likely continue in the dizzying cycle of self-destruction which she has begun. Seeking security and love, she not only has poor role models to follow, but must contend as well with the inexperience of youth and poor coping abilities. Rebellious, she has severed relationships with those who are best equipped to help her. Her future is not optimistic.

There was a time when it seemed that the vicious progression could be interrupted. Aware that my life had changed, Annie was becoming frantic for some real answers to her own problems and was a more-than-willing listener. I shared what Christ had done for me. Admitting her own basic need, she knelt and prayed with me. There were high expectations in both of our hearts, expectations which were shattered some six months later when she announced angrily, "I've tried it your way and it doesn't work!" Somehow, the real message hadn't made it through. She hadn't understood.

Today, Annie lives in the pretense of religion. In the midst of her life-style she talks about being in the Lord's will. While discussing "the Lord's leading" in her life, she will admit that she hasn't opened her Bible in years. In trying to convince her listener that she lives "close to God" she is careful to point out that she doesn't particularly care to be with His people.

Problems seldom just "happen." Annie, Sonia, and Nora walk a path that has been worn deep before them, but a helping hand may assist them to surmount the obstacles that hold them on this road to self-ruin. I walk gently into this dark night of theirs. They are filled with pain, and like wounded birds, they frighten easily. One does not charm birds with loud shouts of alarm, but with patience and love and the building of trust.

CHAPTER EIGHT

Louise

Whenever Richard Cory went down town,
We people on the pavement looked at him:
He was a gentleman from sole to crown,
Clean favored, and imperially slim.

And he was always quietly arrayed,
And he was always human when he talked;
But still he fluttered pulses when he said,
"Good-morning," and he glittered when he walked.

And he was rich—yes, richer than a king—
And admirably schooled in every grace:
In fine, we thought that he was everything
To make us wish that we were in his place.

So on we worked, and waited for the light,
And went without the meat, and cursed the bread;
And Richard Cory, one calm summer night,
Went home and put a bullet through his head.

> E. A. Robinson
> *Richard Cory*

Incest. It's a nasty word. If we think of it at all, we at least prefer to relegate it to the ranks of "inferior" or "lower socio-economic" families. If we can keep the horror confined to the poor and the disadvantaged, our own garments will remain unsoiled. Unfortunately, such is not the case. No one would ever have described my own family as anything but upper middle class, and most respectable. To some, we were rich.

Denied the security of social or economic status, there are those who would seek immunity behind yet another barrier, that of "spirituality." "Certainly," many would insist, "we won't find that sort of a problem within our churches—at least not within the fundamental, Bible-believing denominations." Remember Richard Cory. Things are not always as they seem.

Louise was one of the very first persons to whom I was introduced after I began attending a local, Bible-believing church. We liked each other on sight, and the friendship developed into one of those rare, once-or-twice-in-a-lifetime relationships that allows total communication, no matter how often interrupted by time or distance. Though not a sister in the flesh, she and I are truly sisters in spirit.

Widowed, Louise was doing an obviously excellent job of rearing her two teenaged daughters. Not only did they carry about with them a sense of delightful wholesomeness, but the clearly evident family unity experienced with Louise's in-laws was a joy to behold. Personal interest and involvement were expressed in a multitude of ways, including financial assistance to insure that Darcie, Emilie, and their mother did not lack for any necessity in life.

Although Louise and I were very close, I never found cause or desire to tell her about my experience with my stepfather. Busy exploring the here and now of the other's personality, and occupied with spiritual growth, neither of us was much concerned with the past. Not being letter writers of any great acclaim, the few correspondences that passed between us while I lived out of state were mostly superficial in nature, dealing with present events and personalities. When I returned to town after a long absence I looked forward to resuming our relationship.

Arriving somewhat exhausted, early in the week I first encountered Louise at a Wednesday night prayer meeting at church. She seemed unusually tense, but as she was in the process of moving for the second time in just a few months, it was simple to connect the two in my mind. Sunday morning when I saw her again, however, I realized that the problem was far more serious.

"Need to talk?" I watched her eyes. She lowered them, then nodded her head slightly. "When?"

Tuesday noon I picked her up for lunch. Before we had driven a full block she blurted out, "My father-in-law has molested both of my daughters!" It was as if someone had suddenly stopped a reel of film in the projector. The multitude of thoughts that tumbled chaotically through my head took several minutes to sort out. After thirty years of silence, of being "different," I had made the decision to tell my story. Within months of that decision I was confronted not only with data on Annie and her daughters, but with Louise's compelling need to talk about the experience that had so devastated the lives of her girls and herself. In one flood of emotion I felt both despair and relief. Forgiveness aside, somehow I was no longer quite so "different" as I had been before. The empathy I felt for Darcie, Emilie, and Louise was piercing.

The knowledge was not new for Louise, but some renewed contacts with her father-in-law had stirred painful memories, and she was having trouble dealing with the feelings that were arising out of those memories. In essence, she had not been able to forgive.

Darcie had been about eleven years old, Emilie just a few years younger. Prayer meeting nights were just a bit too long for the girls to manage easily during the school week. Grandpa suggested that Louise and Grandma attend prayer meeting together. He would stay home and take care of the girls.

Before many weeks had passed, Louise noticed some behavioral changes in Darcie. Normally outgoing with her friends, almost to a fault, she suddenly seemed unable to handle herself in the presence of her peers— shy and withdrawn on one occasion, she became boisterous on the next. Louise began to feel uneasy. She reported that on several occasions she felt an "urgency" to get home as soon as possible, only to find the girls neatly tucked into bed and Grandpa sitting in the living room, calmly watching television.

Never content to entrust the education of her children to others, especially in moral and spiritual matters, Louise spent time with each daughter nearly every evening just before they retired. As Darcie was nearing puberty, Louise used the time, and the open channels of communication, to instruct her concerning the facts of life and her own sexuality. One evening, as Louise explained the principles concerning the sanctity of the body and the desirability of purity, Darcie burst into tears, flinging herself into her mother's arms.

When Darcie was again coherent, Louise questioned her gently. Grandpa had been "taking care" of the girls, all right. As soon as he was alone with them, he would take Darcie into the bedroom. Lying on the bed, he would expose himself and encourage his young charge to fondle him, while he would kiss, caress and fondle her. Frightened and ridden with guilt, Darcie kept their "little secret" until she could bear it no more.

Grandpa, of course, denied the charge. Louise had faith in her daughter, and for weeks and months they not only discussed the details of what had happened, but the fact that Darcie was not guilty—it was Grandpa who had sinned. When Darcie expressed concern because "sometimes what he did made me feel good," Louise used the opportunity not only to dispel guilt, but to explain the proper use and place of these "feelings" in the marriage relationship, as a God-given gift, not to be misused.

Recently, Darcie was married. Before the wedding Louise questioned her daughter about her feelings toward a sexual relationship. Darcie's winning smile gave away the answer before the words were out of her mouth. "Mom, I'm really looking forward to it. I love Jeff, and this will be one more way to express it." From the post-honeymoon glow on the faces of both bride and groom, it became evident that she had spoken the truth.

If that were the entire solution to the problem we could smile and rest assured that we had found at least a cure for the effects of incest. There is more, however.

After Darcie revealed the problems she had experienced with her grandfather, Louise went to Emilie. With careful questioning, she satisfied herself that Grandpa had not engaged in any sexual activity with the younger daughter. Several years later reference was made to the incident between Darcie and Grandpa in Emilie's presence. "That happened to me, too," was Emilie's retort.

Louise was dumbfounded. "Why didn't you tell me when I asked you?"

"I don't know. I guess I was ashamed at first. Then I resented the time that you spent with Darcie, but I was too ashamed to admit that I lied."

Grandpa had not molested Emilie to the same extent as he had Darcie, but the damage had had years to fester. Outwardly friendly and obedient, Emilie kept herself apart from most very close relationships. Unrest and a quiet sort of rebellion are the hallmarks of her life. Louise did what she could, but the wounds are deep, made so by Emilie's own nurturing of them. They will take longer to heal, and that will only take place when she allows the lines of communication to be reopened. Louise stands ready and waiting for that day.

What about Grandpa? Financially well-to-do, he and his wife had celebrated several decades of apparently happy anniversaries. Both were viewed by many within the church as examples of all that Christianity can be. They weathered their share of stormy trials but always seemed to rise again to continue on. That was their public life.

Privately, there were vague complaints of "sexual incompatibility" and the divulging to Louise of some of the intimate details of that incompatibility. On several occasions Louise was embarrassed by too-intimate embraces. When she resisted, Grandma would be quick to come to his defense with, "Oh, let him have his little hugs. They make him so happy." She seemed to be totally unaware that there was any kind of a problem.

Grandpa's own father was an alcoholic, and abusive. His mother, terrified by the man she had married, retreated into a shell of passive detachment, unable to assist her child either physically or emotionally. We are forced, once again, to return to the theme of the abused child becoming an abusing adult.

Why the difference between Darcie and Emilie? It is difficult to know the total answer, and yet there are some important clues. To begin with, Darcie admitted that she had a problem; Emilie did not. One cannot treat what one does not know exists, or what one does not acknowledge.

Perhaps even Emilie does not know the real reason that she denied being molested. It may have had something to do with being younger than Darcie when their father died, or the fact that she was younger when the molestation took place. It may have been something totally different. The effects of the total experience are not as disabling as they were in Annie's case and in mine. Their immediate family situation has been infinitely more supportive. Most people would describe Emilie only as "extremely independent." Only those who know her well sense anything more.

Louise believed her children, and she protected them. Once Darcie revealed the molestation, Grandpa never had another opportunity to be alone with either of the girls for even a few minutes. Louise could have chosen to prosecute, but that would have put her children through some painful, public disclosures. Though he never admitted his guilt, Louise threatened him with legal action if he ever again dared to touch either of them.

Darcie was able to vent every feeling that she had about the relationship with her grandfather. Guilt, shame and humiliation evaporated in an atmosphere of love and understanding. But Emilie was able to reveal very little of her experience. She still carries those negative feelings inside of herself.

We cannot evaluate the standing of another in the eyes of God. That Louise's father-in-law sinned is clearly evident from Scripture, but whether or not he is truly born again is a matter between him and the Lord. He says that he is. Had he admitted what he did, it would have been extremely helpful to both of the girls. It certainly would have been spiritually helpful to himself. It would not, however, have been enough to solve the problems that his sin brought to pass.

"Praying about it" is insufficient of itself, but the humanistic approaches to the problem that leave God out of the equation often allow for a kind of morality that brings its own emotional turmoil. What many of those approaches do recognize, however, is that the problems of incest simply do not disappear spontaneously. Weeks and months, sometimes years, are needed to sort through the consequences of the degradation that assails every person involved with an incestuous affair. Prayer helps, yes. God's contribution to our problem-solving is never to be discounted, but we must go beyond, "I'm sorry, it will never happen again" or "Okay, I forgive you." Just because we are Christians, we are not immune to emotional disturbances, and we must work to resolve the issues within ourselves.

Louise has come a long way since that day we first discussed the problem. Concerned with her daughters, she had been unable to find proper ventilation of her own feelings. Once she was able to discuss them it was like applying medication to a wound. We can now, jokingly, refer to her "mother-bear syndrome." Our last discussion which included the incest topic revealed a growing sense of freedom from her feelings of resentment.

CHAPTER NINE

Families That Hurt

Dove-voices with a dying fall
Cooed desolation
Answering grief by grief.

Only the serpent in the dust,
Wriggling and crawling,
Grinned an evil grin, and thrust
His tongue out with its fork.

Christina Rossetti
Eve

As the horror of the scope of incest began to unfold in the early eighties, legal authorities and social agencies were at a loss to know how to deal with a problem that seemed to be growing faster than quack grass. Early estimates of the extent of the problem ranged anywhere between 3% and 50% of the female population of the United States. Women who had been silent for years about their childhood experiences with incest finally found the courage to reveal what had happened to them and seek help, but these reports further confused an already unclear picture. Researchers had still not learned how to accurately sort the enormous amount of information they were receiving.

Nearly ten years later, in a still concerned but more rational atmosphere, most researchers place the figure for females at somewhere around one in four who are sexually assaulted before they reach the age of eighteen; approximately one in six boys is exploited before that same age. Eighty percent of those victims knew and trusted their attackers.[1] The total number of children who are victimized in this country in any given year is probably somewhere between 60,000 and 100,000.[2]

More accurate research and greater cooperation by the media have helped the public to understand that incest is defined by sexual contact between family members, whether they be blood-related or not, and that actual intercourse need not take place before serious psychological damage occurs. Television productions, such as *Something About Amelia,* have alerted the general public that help is available for victims, and gone are "nice" little terms such as *intra-family child sexual abuse,*[3] which try to civilize a horrifying act. The emotional wreckage that remains in the wake of incest is clear evidence that it represents a violation, not just *by* a trusted person, but *of* a personhood.

Physical acts occurring in incest cover the entire scope of man's depraved imagination, and the research does not make pleasant reading. Surprisingly, penetration is often not accomplished, but both oral and anal sex are frequent, as is interfemoral "intercourse" and digital penetration. Mutual masturbation and petting are common. For our purposes, further details are not necessary; it is enough to know that the facts are ugly.

If penetration is often not accomplished, obviously rape or actual intercourse is not the usual beginning of an incestuous affair. Researchers agree, and as far back as 1979, Robert Geiser reported, "There is usually a progression of sexual contact over a considerable period of time. Most commonly it begins with exhibitionism.

This leads eventually to masturbation, mutual masturbation, and other fondling."[4] In cases which *are* initiated by rape, the victim, of course, must deal with the trauma of violence as well as that of the subsequent incest.

Very few incestuous "affairs" are one-time-only contacts. Some last for two or three years, others continue for as long as the daughter continues to live in the home, often stretching over a twelve- or thirteen- year period of time. Most are difficult to bring to a close.

Perpetrators use coercion, threats, subtle courting (which the victim usually does not connect to the consequence), or simply sneaking into a daughter's bed, to produce the desired response from their victims. They seldom, it would appear, consider the long-term effects of their actions.

Incest is not an individual problem; it is a matter of dysfunctional families. As one expert notes:

> Overt incest is evidence in itself of gross parental psycho-pathology as of defective family structure. Father-daughter incest is commonest, . . . but both parents are involved in any form of incest pattern, because it is very difficult for one spouse "not to know" of such a relationship within the family. Incest may represent a pattern that serves to maintain a tenuous equilibrium.

> For instance, in daughter-father incest, the daughter often fulfills many of the mother's functions, the latter having withdrawn from parental tasks, often to work outside the home. But the parents maintain a facade of role competence, and after the "discovery" of incest behavior such families often break up.[5]

Each member of the family has an important role to play in the tragedy of incest, and the victim or victims, along with father, mother, and siblings, characteristically guards those roles jealously. Not to do so would destroy the family, as seventeen-year-old Kim discovered.

After twelve years of abuse, Kim's fears exploded into a nightmare as she watched her father's growing "affection" for her twelve-year-old sister, Joyce. Only recently having found the strength to say "no" to his frequent assaults on her own body, she was not willing to again offer herself in exchange for the new target of his attention. Another sister, Lisa, had been victimized at the same time as Kim, so she knew that the threat was very real—"Daddy's" relationship with Joyce would progress as far as he could convince his newest victim to go. Kim took the only action she could think of—she told a school counselor.

Action was quick. The authorities stepped in and removed her father from the home. A trial followed, and "Daddy" was sentenced to prison. All were to receive counseling. Unfortunately, although action was quick, treatment was less that decisive. Counseling was brief and superficial at best, and soon Kim's grandmother, mother and two sisters were blaming her for family division and the loss of her father's career. While Lisa admitted to some abuse, Joyce denied that her father had done anything unseemly. Family pressuring tactics were effective, and soon Kim, against her will, found herself writing letters begging that her father be allowed to return to his family.

Now Lisa makes frequent attempts at suicide, and Kim lives away from home. By her own choice, she visits rarely and briefly. While she has finally resolved her feelings for the weak, passive mother who preferred to allow sexual misconduct rather than confront and stop it, she is torn by her feelings for her sisters who alternately reject her and confide in her. She professes disgust for her father, except when he seems to make progress in personal development—he has expressed a desire to learn to read and thinks that going to church might help. Then she glows with excitement and pride, demonstrating additional inner conflict over the whole situation. What she really wants from them is acceptance and love, things which they seem incapable of providing to anyone until they deal with their basic problem of self-esteem.

Contrary to popular belief, the incestuous family is not necessarily the lower socio-economic or even the over-crowded family, although they must bear their share of the blame. These families are, however, more likely to come in contact with authorities upon discovery and become part of the statistics. Only rarely do sensational cases of well-to-do executives make the headlines. They are more often handled "privately."

Often patriarchal in nature, such homes frequently have an almost tangible aura of violence. Many incestuous families are far too socially isolated to receive any support against eruptions of this violence, and the children are often physically as well as sexually abused. They come from all walks of life: from ghettos and mansions, from churches and barrooms, from farms as well as from cities.

The mothers in these families are key figures. Frequently abused and emotionally deprived as children, they tend to have married early as an escape. Their unfortunate affinity for abusive husbands causes many to become passive and detached in an effort to avoid the physical and emotional pain that surrounds them. In a significant number of cases, sexual withdrawal has taken place preceding the incest event.[6] Seldom is she totally unaware of what is happening between her daughter and her husband, an element in their abuse which often makes it more difficult for some daughters to forgive their mothers than to forgive their fathers.

Kim's mother would "creep" up the stairs toward the

bathroom, where her husband and daughter were occupied, softly calling her daughter's name, but only after sufficient time had elapsed for the abuse to take place. He would emerge from the bathroom, explaining that Kim (or Lisa—he took turns) was taking a bath and that he had to use the toilet. She never admitted to any knowledge of the abuse.

Some mothers actively enourage the incest:

> It may be very open, as the mother who bluntly says to her daughter, "Tonight it is your turn to sleep with your father." Sometimes it is more subtle, as the mother who leaves her daughter sitting on the father's lap when she goes out and calls back over her shoulder to the girl as she leaves, "Now take good care of Daddy while I'm gone."[7]

Most mothers, however, are not that calculated in their responses. "Most studies suggest that while the mother may not allow the fact of the incest into the conscious awareness, she is most often aware of it on a preconscious level."[8] Had the mother been strong enough to acknowledge the incest, she might have been able to prevent it from occurring in the first place.

Sometimes facilitated by the mother's physical absence from the home, the "mother" role assumed by the child makes her an allowable sex partner in the eyes of her poorly-restrained father. Almost invariably, some sort of alienation between mother and daughter has occurred before the incest.

Marge and Annie are both perfect examples of these powerful denial systems at work. Marge at first was outraged when she was informed of my stepfather's actions toward me, but then she began to consider the consequence of continued belief. She used the first defense offered to support denial. To ask for details would have been far too risky; it would have proved the charges. Even today, she conveniently "forgets" the facts which she learned in our confrontation only a few short years ago.

Annie simply preferred not to know. In a moment of unburdening she admitted that when Dan was drunk he would often "climb into bed with the girls," but she denied any knowledge of what happened while he was there. She made it a point not to know. Knowing would have required action on her part.

While the mother is an important figure in the incestuous family, the question that comes to the minds of many readers is, "What kind of a man would want to have sex with his own daughter?"

The person seen in public often proves to be quite different in private, in the context of his own home. Frequently perceived as a "good provider" for his family, the perpetrator of incest is many times viewed by the community as one of its "pillars." Many of these men have been abused or deprived as children themselves; their public appearance masks the insecurity and depression that have followed them through the years.[9]

Some are physically abusive; others exploit their power through verbal attacks. Most are characterized by poor impulse control. They are not sex perverts or "dirty old men." Rather, they commonly are somewhere in their late thirties and, as mentioned earlier, may have experienced sexual alienation from their wives. Kim is only one among thousands who bitterly charge, "If Mom would have done her job, I wouldn't have had to." The abusive father figure is lonely, frustrated, out of control, and has a distorted view of reality.

Often desperately disgusted with himself, the man who commits incest is often searching for love and acceptance long denied him. Most likely, he would have preferred being a good father, and he is miserable in his failure.

Why does a man commit incest? In twenty-five years I lost count of the number of times I asked that question. I never found an answer. Neither, it would seem, has anybody else, least of all, the perpetrators. Their letters, in response to a short article I wrote for a religious publication, express their bewilderment, sometimes exceeding that of their victims. Some were imprisoned for their crime. Some were in a prison of another kind— that of family rejection and social ostracism. Most were sorry. The belligerent ones, of course, don't write. "I was drunk" or "I was out of my head" sometimes appear, but not as often as one would expect.

At some point, almost all try to place the blame on their victims. "She asked for it" is an excuse, not a reason. It is also, probably, a lie. One can scarcely hold a child of eight responsible for seduction. Looking back on my own seventh- and eighth- grade pictures, I rest assured that my "seductiveness" was not a motivating factor.

> The sexually abusive father does not use the child primarily for sexual gratification but principally as a means of reconfirming and discharging his low self-worth. He approaches his child sexually without full awareness of the needs, drives and motives fueling his behavior, nor of its consequences to his child, family and himself.[10]

Some men see their families as possessions and may well reason that they can do as they please with what they own.

No matter what the rationalization, no matter how "all right" the action may appear, they all know at some level that what they are doing is wrong. They all insist upon keeping "our little secret."

Even therapy doesn't help to solve the mystery. Larry, who had undergone treatment for sexually abusing his three daughters, was of special interest to me. Surely he would be able to shed light on the mystery.

Mildly surprised that I found him not only cooperative, but likeable, I was disappointed in his response. "Why?" was the one question he could not answer. "I don't know why I did it. I don't even remember the oldest one. That hurts her, and I'm sorry, but I guess I was just too drunk. With the other two, I know that I was scared and I hated what I was doing, but I couldn't stop. It was almost a relief when I was caught."

The man who can identify real causes for incestuous behavior is an exception. I have never met one.

We make no attempt to exonerate the men who commit incest—their crime is horrendous—but we do realize that they are hurting, confused individuals whose own needs have been long neglected.

The picture of the victim is less distinct than that of her parents, and she asks the only question more difficult to answer than "Why?"—"Why me?" The answer is equally elusive. Some are unusually attractive, or bear a resemblance to their mothers which creates a recognition factor that breaks down barriers; some acquire a certain seductive manner with their emerging sexuality during puberty. These same factors, however, are often present in girls who are not victimized, and many who are more attractive, or more like their mothers, or more seductive never have the problem. Some are small children or infants who possess none of these qualities.

Ranging in age from a few months to late teens, the oldest daughter seems to run a slightly greater risk of becoming a victim, although younger sisters of victims are at high risk, especially if no disclosure was made of the first incest. A daughter with special problems, physical or mental, is also particularly vulnerable. Mary De Young notes that stepdaughters are 150% more likely to be victimized than natural-born daughters, a statistic that tends to be viewed by "the community in general and the helping professions in particular ... with less alarm and discomfort, [but] the incest victims of stepfathers rarely share that benevolent attitude."[11]

The response of victims varies greatly. Some, especially those who have been victimized as small children, enjoy the experience, even learning to initiate episodes, until they find out that it is wrong. This realization comes when they try to talk about what happens when they are "alone with Daddy," or when they stop to consider that this particular activity must always be kept secret. Some relish the attention and affection they receive—something is better than nothing. Others find themselves drowning in a rising sea of fear and hatred, unable to utter a cry for help. Some actually believe that they are holding their families together. When one considers the aftermath of most disclosures, this assumption may have some degree of validity, but they support a false unity, and the price is always far too high.

Most girls are simply unable to say "no." The father figure is simply too overwhelming an obstacle to refuse. Some have been led by their perpetrators to believe that they are responsible for the incest, and they are disabled by guilt. Because of the complex family relationships involved, the daughter often feels worthless, helpless, and isolated within the confines of her isolated family.

At the same time, many victims experience a sense of power. Role reversal with her mother and the power to reveal or not reveal "the secret" are heady commands for a young girl. They can only add to the burdens she already bears.

Psychological damage to the victim as a result of incest is difficult to assess. Often, she behaves sexually in her relationships with men: flirting, enticing, becoming promiscuous. Just as often, she withdraws from all heterosexual relationships. One daughter associates emotion with sex and expresses herself sexually as a matter of habit; the other sees heterosexual contact as the source of all her misery and turns from it. Sometimes both reactions occur within the same family. *Ms.* magazine states that 75% of the adolescent prostitutes interviewed in a Minneapolis study reported that they had been victims of incest.[12] The same article reports a high percentage of adolescent drug addicts as having been involved in some form of family sexual abuse, and names sexual abuse as a significant factor in adolescent runaways.

The damage is not just a temporary injury that the victim will "get over" with time. Results are often lifelong, with tragic consequences, and the importance of counseling to help adult survivors overcome the reverberations of their experience is nowhere more clear than in the case of Lori.

Her childhood was marred by sexual activity with her father, who, although he did not physically penetrate her body, left an indelible impression on her mind. Lori married early to escape her home life, choosing a man who was both physically weak and emotionally indecisive. They had two children, a boy and a girl.

When her daughter was about six years old, Lori revealed the fact of her molestation to a brother and sister-in-law. Before the day was over, word of that conversation had reached her father. Before the week was over, he had arrived on her doorstep and raped her, threatening to do the same to her daughter if he were reported.

Feeling even more helpless now than she did as a

child, she was unable to stop the attacks. "After he leaves each night," she said, "I scrub myself in a hot shower for as long as I can, knowing I can never really feel clean again." Already desperate and suicidal, she panicked when the next shock came: she was pregnant with no clue as to whose baby she was carrying—her husband's or her father's.

Desperately ill with a pregnancy that would have been difficult even in more favorable circumstances, she finally visited a psychiatrist who hospitalized her immediately, called in her husband, who had been at work during the attacks, and explained the situation to him. Fortunately, he not only understood the facts of her predicament, but he provided the emotional support that Lori so badly needed.

She has received what therapy she can afford, and once her father found out that she was pregnant, he stopped his visits. "But," she says, "prosecution isn't worth the trouble. He wouldn't be imprisoned long enough to protect my daughter until she grows up." He has, meanwhile, called to suggest that perhaps he is the one who should introduce his granddaughter, now eight years old, to sex. Consider the following:

WARNING!

If you are contemplating rape (and the majority of rapes are planned), be sure to check the statutory penalties for this crime in your state. Usually the most severe penalties are reserved for raping your neighbor's wife (20 years to life). The punishment is less severe (up to 10 years) for raping your neighbor's *child*. The penalty is even less (up to five and above years) for raping your *own child.* . . .[13]

Lori's nightmare will continue until her father's death. Her fears are well founded, and so is her despair.

Kim's father, after abusing two daughters for twelve years, was sentenced to a year and a half in prison. He served less than six weeks of that term.

Part of the problem is that we often treat the symptoms and not the disease. Just as measles is not a rash but an illness for which a rash is one symptom, incest, sexual abuse, is not the disease; it is a symptom of disease—that of the dysfunctional family. As long as adults try to meet adult needs through their children rather than seeking proper avenues of release, and as long as adults fail to seek proper solutions to their problems, the disease will manifest its ugly "symptom" of sexual depravity.

Untreated, it will multiply itself. Simply stopping the abuse is like applying Calamine lotion to a measles' rash; the immediate itch may be taken care of, but the disease remains untreated and highly contagious.

Fortunately, some communities are beginning to recognize this fact and are taking steps to make sure that properly trained, sensitive personnel are employed in programs designed to treat the disease and not just the symptoms, and to make sure that victims and their families don't become lost in a system which causes more damage than good, mere objects to be handled, as Kim's family apparently was.

The psychological needs of newly discovered sexual abuse victims, in some localities, is becoming part of training for interns. Counselors who have made the treatment of sexual abuse a special concern in their studies are filling positions in team treatment programs such as Project Harmony in Grand Rapids, Michigan, and The National Children's Advocacy Center in Huntsville, Alabama.

While in some areas of the country, new treatment methods will be of great assistance to young victims, our job is to insure that things keep on getting better in more places, and to let victims know where help is available and that somebody cares.

If the proper authorities can be educated to see the total picture of incest realistically, victims need not be further victimized, and perhaps the vicious cycle can be stopped. Healing can take place. In the face of chaos, perhaps the house divided can be made whole.

CHAPTER TEN

From "Dear Daddy" to "Abba Father"

His thoughts said, But the lost years,
what of them?
His Father said, I will restore to thee
the years that the locust hath eaten,
the cankerworm and the caterpillar and
the palmer worm. I know the names of
all the insects and worms which have
devoured thy beauty and thy power. I
will deal with them all, and cause thee
to help others in danger of like injury.
So shall thy years be restored.

Amy Carmichael
Lost Years

From time to time, David is able to talk me into a game of *Monopoly*. Invariably, he lands on both Park Place and Boardwalk before I do, buys them, and loads them up with houses, and I know that my hopes of winning, "just once," have again been dashed. I may survive for a couple of rounds of the board, but even the "Chance" card (advance to Go—collect $200) that allows me to by-pass his high-rent district is only a brief respite. Sooner or later I will land on one of the two properties, and I will lose the game. "Chance" is never a new start; one lives with the consequences of previous rounds.

We live our lives in the light of the accumulation of "previous rounds." Whatever happens, we can't "undo" a single day that we've lived, no matter how much we would like to. Israel's King David learned that lesson the hard way, and the lesson included incest.

Unique in God's plan for Israel, we read of David: "'I have found David son of Jesse a man after my own heart; he will do everything I want him to do.' From this man's descendants God has brought to Israel the Savior Jesus, as he promised" (Acts 13:22, 23).

From the time that he was anointed by Samuel in I Samuel 16 until he saw Bathsheba in 2 Samuel 11, David succeeded. At that point, however, lust triumphed over good sense, and David committed adultery. When Bathsheba announced that she was pregnant, David was desperate to hide the evidence and finally resorted to having her husband killed. God's opinion of what David had done was very clear: "But the thing David had done displeased the Lord" (2 Samuel 11:27b).

In chapter 12, the prophet Nathan confronts David, and David repents. Although the Lord chooses to spare David's life, the king finds that he must live with the consequences of what he has done. Nathan foretells that calamity will descend on the royal household, calamity which will spring from within the house itself. He also tells that the child born of the sinful union will die. Within that chapter, the child is stricken and succumbs. As David comforts Bathsheba, another infant is conceived—Solomon, who will succeed his father to the throne. The first part of the prophecy begins to be fulfilled in the first verse of the next chapter: "In the course of time, Amnon, son of David fell in love with

Tamar, the beautiful sister of Absalom son of David" (2 Samuel 13:1).

Amnon, on the advice of his cousin, Jonadab, arranges to be alone with Tamar and then rapes her. With his lust satisfied, he burns with hatred and has her, literally, locked out of the house. Horrified, Tamar seeks refuge in the house of her brother, Absalom. He tries to comfort her, but it is clear that she has been emotionally destroyed. Verse 20 tells us, "And Tamar lived in her brother Absalom's house, a desolate woman."

If that were the end of the story, it would have been bad enough, but it was merely the beginning. The results of incest seldom stop so short. David's fury apparently did not find expression in any corrective action, and, two years later, Absalom finally takes some decisive action of his own—he has Amnon killed. To realize the importance of his act, we must realize that Amnon was David's eldest son. According to the usual practices of anointing kings, people looked to him as the future king of Israel. While God had chosen Solomon to sit on the throne, that choice seemed to be clear to no one except David, Bathsheba, and the prophet Nathan (1 Kings 1).

Apart from Kileab (or Daniel) who is mentioned only in two genealogies, Absalom was next in the line of succession. Solomon was eighth!

One cannot say whether Tamar's abuse and David's mishandling of that event were the whole cause of Absalom's rebellion, but the violent emotions we read of in the chapters following are understandable in light of them. The capstone of Absalom's rebellion takes place when he openly commits incest with his father's concubines. It almost costs David his kingdom (2 Samuel 15ff.). It does cost Absalom his life, and with him out of the way, Adonijah, son number four, decided to make

an attempt for the throne in David's old age. He, too, loses his life.

David's calamity was of gigantic proportion, but the lessons are clear: God abhors sexual decadence, and the problems arising from it do not go away by themselves. Tamar was as much a victim of David's sin as she was of Amnon's. Like Tamar, we cannot control all of the events that come into our lives. We can, however, control our attitudes toward those events, and we are given biblical precedent to demonstrate that truth.

Much earlier in Israel's history there was a young man who demonstrated the power of proper attitudes. His name was Joseph. His problem did not include incest, but he certainly suffered tremendous abuse. Hated and sold into slavery by his own brothers, he made the best of a terrible situation. Competence, hard work, and positive attitudes brought him to the top job in his master's household. It also brought him to the attention of his master's wife.

It would have been easy for Joseph to justify immorality with Potiphar's mate. Instead, however, he voiced only one concern before he ran out of the house, "How then could I do such a wicked thing and sin against God?"[1] The result of his unflinching obedience to God was imprisonment on a false charge of attempted rape. He did not, as we would expect, decide to hang his head and blame God. Competence, hard work, and positive attitudes again brought him to the top position available to him: he became prison manager. The same qualities eventually brought him to the second highest position in all of Egypt.

When the results of hatred are slavery and jail, revenge could be very sweet. It was several years before Joseph's brothers reappeared on the scene, but when they did we find not the expected vengeful hatred on Joseph's part, but quite the opposite. After some testing to see if his brothers had learned any lessons through what they had done, he joyfully forgave them! "So then, it was not you who sent me here, but God."[2]

Joseph seemed to know the glorious truth about forgiving: it is as much a gift to yourself as it is to the person to whom it is extended, perhaps even greater. In order to hold hatred and resentment, you have to do just that; you have to hold it, remember it, and rehearse it. As you drink the bitter waters of hostility, they will do more damage to your own soul than to the one who has wronged you.

You and I are not victims of circumstance, but the direct objects of God's love. If we allow Him to, God will control the "Chance" cards in our lives.

> And we know that in all things God works for the good of those who love him, who have been called according to his purpose. For those God foreknew he also predestined to be conformed to the likeness of his Son, that he might be the firstborn among many brothers (Romans 8:28, 29).

How can something as vile as incest be the result of God's divine love? Joseph might have asked that same question in regard to his situation. Obedience to God apparently brought him into deeper trouble as he went along, and he could not see the end. He didn't know that he would be the means of keeping his entire family alive. What he *did* know was that God doesn't ask us to understand—He asks us to believe. Joseph acted on that, and thus laid the groundwork for God to forge for Himself a nation.

We must be cautious about drawing too many parallels, certainly. Sin can never be condoned on the grounds that some good could possibly come from it, but from the attitude of forgiveness in the face of great wrong we can glean some positive truths. Forgiveness is

113

the key that can open the door for understanding and sensitivity to the needs of others. It can put into motion the forces that can prevent the plague of incest from reaching into succeeding generations. It can begin to change the direction of an entire family.

Forgiving doesn't come easily. Even when we think we want to forgive, we find ourselves holding onto that last small corner of our resentment, somehow afraid to let it go. Unresolved guilt feelings of our own could be part of the cause. By holding onto the offense, somehow our own guilt doesn't seem quite so bad. It may help to take a good look at those feelings.

The guilt over incest is most often justifiable guilt, and the sources are often quite predictable. "Why didn't I fight?" "Why did I do everything he told me to do?" Because you couldn't do anything else. "What did I do to cause it?" Nothing. A child is not the responsible party in the parent/child relationship.

At six or eight or twelve, most daughters obey, either from training or through fear—and fathers who commit incest do make threats. The conflict that presents itself in such a situation is more than most children are able to handle, even when they know that what they're being asked to do is wrong. Saying "no" isn't always effective, at any rate, as many victims know from experience. "Fighting" isn't even a consideration with a smaller, weaker child, and even in an older child, the psychological barrier against resisting an adult authority figure is almost unbearable. Passiveness, lip-biting, or detachment seem to be the more usual reactions.

"But I sometimes felt good when it was happening." That is not a matter for guilt. That is simply physiology; it's the way you are made. If you are one of those who experienced a degree of pleasure, rest assured that you could no more help "feeling good" than you can help enjoying your favorite music or a nice perfume. All are

114

responses to stimulation of nerve endings. Our bodies were designed to enjoy sexual stimulation.[3] Because that stimulation is out of place does not necessarily prohibit feelings of pleasure. By the same token, pleasure is not able to cancel out the psychological pain that almost invariably follows its misuse.

The ingenuity of the human mind in the creation of false guilt is limitless. Determining whether or not guilt is realistic is sometimes a difficult task, especially when the person you are trying to evaluate is yourself. Outside help is sometimes required to deal effectively with this, as well as other conflicts that arise.

Even brief contact with Scripture informs us that God does not expect us to solve all of our problems by ourselves. We are told in Proverbs 12:15 that "a wise man listens to advice." How grateful I am that I finally discovered the truth of these words!

The decision to write this book was a difficult one, but the resurrection of old memories proved even more difficult. At times I was visibly shaken, and it soon became obvious that I could not continue without support: emotional, to help me to retain a measure of perspective on my life; and editorial, to help me achieve the balance between sensitivity and objectivity that I so desired this manuscript to attain. The Lord brought me to a trained counselor who was also well qualified to advise me concerning editorial matters. Sensitive and perceptive, he did not take long to realize that there were still some unresolved issues relating to my experience.

I entered into counseling with reluctance, but with determination; I would do whatever I had to in order to achieve my goal of producing a publishable manuscript. For the very first time I found myself relating the events of thirty years before. Verbalizing them, however, was more than I could manage at first—they had been locked away for too long. Writing those scenes opened the door to communication, as well as providing a valuable release for some of the feelings that were pent up inside of me.

As we discussed the pages that I had prepared, my counselor and I discovered some of the painful realities of my marriage to Mike. Pushed into the dark recesses of my mind, they were realities that needed resolution. The release that I experienced as I confronted the truth, accepted my own responsibility and "forgave" Mike was a welcome surprise. Tension that I had endured, so long that I was not even aware of it, crumbled like the walls of Jericho, and I knew that the painful price had been worth it. I was ready to begin the manuscript.

It would be gratifying at this point to present a list of counselors who were both sensitive and qualified to deal with the problems of incest. Unfortunately, such a list is not available, although the increased attention that incest is receiving extends that group of counselors able to deal effectively with its particular problems. Recommendation must come through word of mouth, and must be accepted very cautiously.

Humanistic counselors abound. While they do present a degree of relief, they leave God out of the equation as they search for the solutions to dilemmas. Unable to deal with the underlying causes of sin and depravity, and equally unable to assign to God a place within the human experience, they are at best only able to put a Band-Aid on the gaping wound and hope that it will heal sufficiently to prevent it from rupturing at the first blow.

There is another difficulty with the counseling situation that relates to the humanity of both counselor and counselee. When they are members of the opposite sex, the possibility of temptation exists because of the nature of the subject matter. My counselor was most discreet at all times, a quality which I deeply appreciated. At one point during the counseling sessions, I realized that I was very vulnerable. Although there was no wish on my part for personal involvement, there was a sense of helplessness and dependence that would have rendered me defenseless in the event of an imprudent advance. In his book, *Christian Counseling*, Gary Collins states:

> Counseling often involves the discussion of intimate details which would never be discussed elsewhere— especially between a man and a woman who are not married to each other. This can be sexually arousing to both the counselor and counselee. ... Such subtle influences, wrote Freud many years ago, "bring with them the danger of making a man forget his technique and medical task for the sake of a fine experience."[4]

Combined with the attitudes of trust and caring that are present in the counseling situation, the difficulty is at least understandable while it remains unconscionable. Disturbed by my emotions, I was fortunately able to express them. Knowing the cause, in my case, provided the cure. I had been protected by the nature of my counselor's strength. Others have not been quite so fortunate.

Mary De Young states that out of fourteen incest victims questioned, three had been victimized again by the person with whom they were counseling.[5] That information is relayed not to frighten the reader, but to forewarn of possible risks.

Seek out a Christian counselor committed to biblical principles and values. Use only a counselor whom you are able to trust implicitly, but at the same time, remember the dangers inherent in the counseling situation. Should matters get "out of hand" don't forget that you have the right, and the ability, to say "No," or simply to walk out of the room. Sexual abuse by a counselor can undo all of the good that has been accomplished and, if transference has taken place, can be tantamount to an additional incest experience.[6]

No one ever has the right to misuse you sexually, or any other way. The probability factor in counselor/counselee molestation is not overwhelming, but to forego warning would be gross negligence. The benefits of using a male counselor are significant, especially in the areas of transference and building an attitude of trust toward a male figure. You may decide, however, that you would be more confident with a woman.

Victims of incest quite often are more susceptible to sexual molestation by others as well. Many factors could have a bearing on this. It is quite possible to check some of them and change them, thereby reducing the hazards that might lie ahead.

First of all, the reaction of many women to their incest experience is to behave in a provocative manner. Not fully realizing their effect on men, they are literally "asking for it." How do you hold yourself when you talk to a man? Do you find that you behave differently when with a man than with a woman? Do you "drop hints" that you might be available? Ask a friend to help you evaluate these items. A most helpful insight into the way your behavior affects others might be gained by checking a book on body language out of the public library. Work toward correcting any misleading habits that you may have developed.

Avoiding provocative behavior does not mean that you should work to make yourself unattractive. Dressing carelessly, gaining too much weight, or being slovenly about your appearance only project feelings of insecurity. Grooming, neatness and positive attitudes relay a confident spirit.

Second, all too many people (not just incest victims) have an improper view of the demands of the flesh. Just because our bodies, or our emotions, tell us that they want something is no reason to satisfy those demands. People drink too much, gain too much weight and are chained to all manner of bad habits because they have been unwilling to tell their flesh "No." They also wind up with unwelcome sexual involvements. A moment's passion or a passing weakness in this area can bring a lifetime of regrets. The price is too dear.

Our real need is to be loved. No matter what the television commercials and soap operas tell us, no matter what society's values demonstrate, sex and love are not synonymous. Love is a total relationship that works two ways. It is caring, and being cared for; it is understanding and being understood. True love is sensitive to the needs of the other, and it is patient. Love is the kind of trust that enables transparency— allowing the other person to know who you really are with the assurance that rejection is not a possibility. Love is encouraged and encourages, gives and accepts, shares both the joys and the pain of living. Sexuality by itself can never provide any of these things. Like a soap bubble on the wind, the pleasure is too soon gone and leaves only a greater emptiness than before. Sex can happen in a moment; love takes time and effort to develop—but it is worth waiting for.

We get sidetracked. We settle for the lesser things because we have not established the greater ones firmly enough in our minds. Begin to set goals for your life. The old saying is, "If you aim at nothing, you are sure to hit it." It's true: When there is no direction to a life, it is easy to succumb to the temptation to wander. With firm goals, even if they are small to begin with, one can more easily turn aside from the things that might prevent their realization.

Recently I picked up a book entitled, *See You at the Top*, by Zig Ziglar.[7] Designed to help readers toward financial success, it nevertheless deals with other aspects of personal success which are most valuable. Goal setting is one of the areas discussed in detail, and the book is recommended for those who wish to set and achieve personal goals.

Another area dealt with in some detail by Ziglar is that of self-image. Poor self-image is one of the major problems faced by many victims of incest,[8] and poor self-image is one of Satan's greatest lies. Ziglar and I disagree with the idea that Satan is trying to put across—and so does God. From cover to cover, the Bible records God actively involved in the lives of the people He created in His own image. Even though that image has been spoiled by sin, He has not abandoned humankind, but works to restore the relationship that has been marred.

God deals with individuals. Through the pages of the four gospels, we see Christ dealing with a woman married five times and living with a sixth man. A few pages later, we find Christ forgiving a woman caught in the act of committing adultery. In the gospel of Luke He honors a woman who anoints His feet, a woman described as a sinner, a prostitute. He deals with beggars, madmen, thieves, lepers, and rich men. There is only one requirement—each must come repenting of sin and acknowledging Christ as the only salvation.

In learning to identify false guilt, we must also acknowledge that there is a real guilt that we need to deal with, a real guilt that we are helpless to manage by ourselves, or assign to anyone else. It is ours, and ours alone, and no one is exempt from it. Hatred, anger, rebellion and disobedience are all a part of that guilt. But there is One who offers to bear the burden for us; the invitation from the Savior's lips is sweet: "All that the Father gives me will come to me, and whoever comes to me I will never drive away" (John 6:37).

The result of accepting this invitation is overwhelming. "Dear friends, now we are children of God, and what we will be has not yet been made known. But we know that when he appears, we shall be like him, for we shall see him as he is." (1 John 3:2).

A child of God! No matter what our background, no matter what our sin, no matter what our accomplishment or lack of it, by accepting His sacrifice for our guilt we obtain a worth beyond all measure. Worth more than the treasured child of an earthly king, those who accept the invitation of Christ begin a new life that leads to eternity, not worthlessness; a new life that allows God to take charge of the "Chance" cards.

> This is love: not that we loved God, but that he loved us and sent his Son as an atoning sacrifice for our sins (1 John 4:10).

> There is no fear in love. But perfect love drives out fear, because fear has to do with punishment. The one who fears is not made perfect in love. We love because he first loved us (1 John 4:18, 19).

It is possible to deal with all of the other issues involved in incest and miss this, the most important issue of all. Minimally, the job will be more difficult without Christ. The ultimate price exceeds any torment we are able to describe.

There are choices to make. But the circumstances of the past need not dictate the direction of all the tomorrows.

CHAPTER ELEVEN

The Conclusion of It All

But as the girl timidly accosted him, he made a convulsive movement and saved his respectability by a vigorous sidestep. He did not risk it to save a soul. For how was he to know that there was a soul before him that needed saving.

Stephen Crane
Maggie: A Girl of the Streets

Joey was three when I met him. The livid red "wattle" that extended from his chin to his navel pulled his small body into a nearly prenatal position. Somehow one was reminded of a turkey, but there was little thanksgiving connected with his dilemma.

In those days there were no regulations regarding the flammable properties of children's nightwear, so when he found the book of matches and began to play with them while his mother was busy in the kitchen, the damage was almost predictable. By the time he reached his mother, the flames had eaten away a good portion of the skin on his chest and neck. His life had hung in the balance for several days, but, with multiple surgeries, the prognosis was that he would someday approach normal appearance.

Joey and I were in the same hospital. He was between surgeries (three had already taken place), and I had to wait for an infection to clear before an operation of my own could be pursued. The hospital was very small, and once we met, the tiny tyrant would daily demand to be carried to my room. Snuggled beside me on the bed, he would watch television and talk, and it wasn't long before we grew to love each other. Joey hated two things—surgery and fire. My upcoming surgery was a threat to him, and at least once a day he would announce his intention of burning down the operating room, along with its usual occupants, so that they could not perform their work on me.

Joey must be twenty-six now. He probably doesn't care for surgery any more than he did back then, but he is also probably very grateful for the ones that took place. Although they were painful, they restored him. Every person who worked with Joey during those terrible days caused pain that was motivated by love and concern. He knows a truth that too many people miss altogether: sometimes, love hurts.

The victim of incest needs to learn the truth that Joey learned. The pain of disclosure can often seem to be greater than the incest itself, but without that necessary surgery, there can be little hope for healing and wholeness; without disclosure, the deformity can ruin the lives of all that it touches.

The results of disclosure will vary according to the status of the affair. If the incest is ongoing, discovery of the fact may create what appears to be a holocaust. Every family member can emotionally "explode" in a different direction, and all at the same time. Pain, fear, humiliation, and anger do not combine for reasonable discussion. Accusations, both true and false, may be made; accusations of lying or of seduction, accusations that attempt to place the blame on other shoulders, accusations involving the complicity of other family members. Painful details will have to be communicated, and it may be necessary for the family to be separated for a while. Even if the incest has ceased before the disclosure, the results may not be less chaotic if the victim is still living at home.

If the victim is no longer at home, the psychological pain of disclosure will still, undoubtedly, be tremendous. Painful decisions will have to be made in order to determine the proper action. The perpetrator will not seek help on his own, and there may be others in the home who might be spared victimization if disclosure is made. Gratitude for such action will not be soon apparent. As in Joey's situation, however, the temporary pain can be the forerunner of health; it can be the corrective surgery for incest. At times it will seem that anesthetic is in short supply, but the results can be well worth the price. They may turn a house divided into a house reunited in an atmosphere of safety and love.

Some cases, unfortunately, can never be resolved completely. Health problems, mental problems, or uncommon circumstances could present an insurmountable barrier to disclosure on the level we have been discussing. The importance of disclosure on a personal level, discussing the problem with an understanding confidant, cannot be too strongly stressed in these instances. There may be a far better chance for family healing with such counseling, even though it would not be the same as full disclosure, and there is certainly a more optimistic outlook for the victim and the lives she will affect for all of the days to come.

Would-be helpers of incestuous families would do well to keep in mind that those involved are, as a rule, expert in one area—that of secret-keeping. Often the victim is convinced that she alone is responsible for the cohesiveness of her family. Unable to bear the pain of the incest, and equally unable to bear the pain of telling, she may send out clear signals as to the nature of her problem and then, at least initially, deny that a problem exists. There are several indicators that sexual abuse is taking place within a family. Though any one of them could be a sign of a different, nonsexual, problem, genuine suspicion should be reported to the proper authorities. The following list offers possible signs of such abuse:

—The young person tells you that he/she has been sexually abused.
—There is a sudden change in the young person's behavior or achievement.
—The young person becomes severely withdrawn, cutting herself/himself off from peers and adults.
—The young person primarily relates to the other sex in a seductive or sexual manner.
—The young person exhibits unusual fear or hatred of the opposite sex, parents or parent figures.
—The young person either runs away from home or frequently expresses a desire to leave home.
—The young person exhibits unusually mature appearance and behavior and/or reports assuming extreme responsibilities at home.
—The young person's drug abuse or prostitution may indicate sexual abuse.
—The young person talks of being unsafe in his/her own home.
—The young person has unexplainable complaints of physical problems such as stomachache, bladder infection, soreness of the genital area, sleep disturbances, self-mutilation, sore throat.[1]

Although the dynamics of incestuous families have been discussed in a previous chapter, those principles need to be reiterated. The following list relates primarily to physical rather than sexual abuse, but there is sufficient correlation to make it a valuable guide for sensing areas of difficulty, especially when used in conjunction with the previous list concerning victims. Physical abuse is also a reportable offense, and its victims, too, must often rely on outside assistance to bring their silent terror to an end.

1. As a child, was the parent repeatedly beaten or deprived?
2. Does the parent have a record of mental illness or criminal activities?
3. Is the parent suspected of physical abuse in the past?
4. Is the parent suffering lost self-esteem, social isolation, or depression?
5. Has the parent experienced multiple stresses, such as marital discord, divorce, debt, frequent moves, significant losses?
6. Does the parent have violent outbursts of temper?
7. Does the parent have rigid, unrealistic expectations of the child's behavior?
8. Does the parent punish the child harshly?
9. Does the parent see the child as difficult and provocative (whether or not the child is)?
10. Does the parent reject the child or have difficulty forming a bond with the child?
11. Are there currently excessive stresses in the family or parent's life?[2]

Getting involved will not be pleasant. The people you will be dealing with will cry and be angry and hurt, especially if the authorities must become involved. They may seek to find release for these emotions on you. You may try to make your report anonymously, but that may be impossible because of your relationship to the victim or other family members. Most states provide immunity from prosecution when a report is made in good faith, and they assume that anyone reporting is doing so in good faith.

There need be little fear of being led to believe a false report. A child's rehearsal of abuse is sufficient evidence for a bona fide report. If a child or teen tells you that she is being victimized incestuously, assume that the report is true. The instances of false reports are so scant as to be almost negligible. The coordinator of suspected childhood sexual abuse in one large city stated that he had never found a case of a natural child lying about such treatment.[3] The rate for adopted children is less than 10%. Incest is a serious charge. It is not made lightly. Many children and young teens do not even have the concepts or language to make up such stories, and must report through the use of anatomically correct dolls.

In most communities, Protective Services is the agency to which one reports a case, or a suspected case, of incest. Their immediate concern is the protection of the child. Whether or not you are in agreement with current legal procedures in your area, this agency is best suited to deal with the immediate concerns of incest.

Some people are required by law to report the abuse of any person under 18 years of age—doctors, teachers, social workers, school counselors and others in the "helping" professions. There is a moral obligation for others, however, one that cannot easily be ignored. Should you be the one to discover, or even suspect incest, you could be the only hope for a child's nightmare to come to an end. You could be the only hope for a family to be healed. Separating or splitting a family in such circumstances is really not a consideration when the unity they display is a pseudo-unity, built on the destruction of a child's life.

Beyond reporting, the possibility of continued involvement will vary considerably. Much depends on the attitudes of the family. The following suggestions may be practical in some situations.

The victim will most likely be suffering from a poor self-concept. The incest itself is cause enough; the turmoil of disclosure will do little to help, especially if the mother is not able to be supportive. Let the victim know that you are still her friend and available to help her and to listen to her. She does not need additional feelings of rejection at this time.

The mother will need assistance. If the father is imprisoned, there will be family support factors to consider, and acute embarrassment that neighbors, relatives, and people at church "know," whether or not they actually do. For professing Christians, the shame at discovery of the "family secret" can be even worse. Do not assume that the authorities have provided information for assistance. They probably haven't. Help the mother, if necessary, to make contact with the appropriate agencies for legal, financial and emotional aid. Help her, if possible, to see how imperative it is for her to be supportive of the victim. Above all, be ready to listen as she gets rid of some of her own frustrations. Her world has fallen apart and she will need someone to stand with her as she works to put it back together again.

Get rid of your own mental images. The pictures formed when incest is the issue are not pretty, and they can inhibit your ability to be of real help. The victim needs to tell her story, to release the pent-up details and frustrations that she has kept hidden so long, but the real task is building for the future, not remembering the past. The father who admits his sin needs help to rejoin his family, and that will only happen where negative attitudes have been avoided.

Frequently, incest is not revealed until the victim has reached maturity. There is nothing to be gained by reporting to the authorities. In most cases, the victim is past the age where the agencies have any jurisdiction. Again, however, she probably needs to talk. Learn to listen. Learn to keep confidential information to yourself—no "prayer requests" to anyone! Your attitudes of understanding are essential, not your reactions of shock. Above all, know your own limitations, and know when to recommend professional assistance in counseling.

Work to help the victim realize some of the attitudes presented in earlier chapters of this book. Proper self-image and sense of worth in the eyes of others and of God, proper attitudes toward guilt, both false and real, and proper attitudes toward forgiveness are all important. Above all, make sure that she understands that the greatest help of all lies in becoming a true child of God. Therein lies a source of strength not available through others.

If you are presently caught in the trap of incest, tell someone. No matter who you are, no matter what you feel about your responsibility in the matter, no matter what you think you may deserve—you do not deserve incest. You are not doing your family or yourself any favors by keeping the secret, and you may be paving the way for incalculable harm in the years and the generations to come. It will be tough going for a while—disclosure is never easy, but assistance has improved in the thirty years since I tried to tell what happened to me. If you do not feel that you can tell your mother, then remember that a teacher, a school nurse, a doctor or dentist, a school counselor or a social worker are usually required by law to report sexual abuse when they learn of it. You can even contact Protective Services yourself. If you are ignored the first time, then tell someone else, but don't let what is happening to you continue.

If you have been victimized, but the actual incest has stopped, then seek help for the unresolved conflicts that you have. You cannot bury them successfully without resolving them, for they will come back as unwelcome ghosts to haunt you.

Through some YWCA groups an organization now exits which has given us a name, AMAC, Adults Molested as Children. It is designed to help those who have been through experiences similar to our own to discover that they are not alone, and, through discussion, discover one more path to healing and emotional health.

Sexual abuse is not the only abuse that lives around us. The statistics are horrifyingly low in comparison to the actual cases. One fact is clear—abused children grow up to be abusing parents unless someone intervenes. That means that unless we become personally involved, the statistics will become even more shocking.

Look around you. Do you see any families that are isolated and lonely? Your friendship could be the very thing that prevents them from exploding into abuse. Do you see families who seem to be having a difficult time coping? As you give of yourself, teaching them new ways to deal with their frustrations, you can love them into the Christian community. You can help to put them into a position where they can start to build strengths into their lives, to build their house upon a rock.

Therefore everyone who hears these words of mine and puts them into practice is like a wise man who built his house on the rock. The rain came down, the streams rose, and the winds blew and beat against that house; yet it did not fall, because it had its foundation on the rock. But everyone who hears these words of mine and does not put them into practice is like a foolish man who built his house on sand. The rain came down, the streams rose, and the winds blew and beat against the house, and it fell with a great crash (Matthew 7:24–27).

Much earlier I spoke of the sense of loss we all experience, the something missing that can never be replaced. We know it in different ways: the pain of watching a child in a healthy, loving father/daughter relationship and knowing that such a relationship can never be ours, the twinge of hurt that comes with the smell of a certain after-shave lotion, or the revulsion at the sight of a certain color, especially if worn by a man. Perhaps the use of a certain word or phrase resurrects the pain. Amy Carmichael spoke of those feelings through the pain she sensed in the orphaned children of India with whom she worked:

> His thoughts said, There are some things that I cannot forget.
>
> His Father said, The humbling memory will help thee to walk slowly with Me and tenderly with others. . . .[4]

Caring is costly. It involves time and energy and personal involvement. Sometimes it is painful and inconvenient. Christ knows that. He cared and was involved enough to leave heaven for our sakes. He gave his time and his energy. He was inconvenienced—all the way to the cross. The result of his caring was new life. The result of our caring can be a new outlook.

THE BOX

On my dresser is a small walnut-stained wooden box. Measuring about 4″ x 5″, it has obviously been hand crafted, and although I have some ideas about who made it, I'm not really sure. It was my stepfather's, and it seemed to be important to him. As a teenager, I stole quarters from it to buy cigarettes. I found it very satisfying to have him unwittingly support a habit that he did not approve of for me.

The contents of the box are as important as the box itself:

one child's ring, pushed back into shape, birthstone missing, somehow the symbol of all my loneliness and misery as a child. It was given to me as a fourth grader, after I had heard the conversation about my stepparents wanting to adopt Annie but willing to find a "good home" for me. It came with the stipulation that if I didn't take care of it, I would never get another. I hated the color of the stone. I bit the soft gold (the stone fell out by itself), and found out that they were right. I never got another ring of my own until I became engaged.

two wedding rings—one gold man's ring, and one woman's ring from which the stones have been removed. The latter looks skeletal, which is not entirely inappropriate. A marriage was dying, a husband is dead, and I was as helpless to revive the one as I was to raise the other.

one picture, torn into small pieces and then taped back together. It shows my stepfather, my sister, and me. His right hand is cupping one of my breasts. I am desperately trying, with one hand, to pull his arm away; my other hand is clenched into a fist. Standing in the background is my birth father. My stepmother took the picture.

Ten years ago, when I challenged God to make something good come out of my incest experience, out of the life I had lived before I became His child, I never dreamed that any of these objects could have any positive meaning for me. Humanistically speaking, I was right. Now that box is one of the most precious objects that I own. In case of fire, it will be the thing I reach for as I leave my apartment.

It represents where I've been, and what I could have become. It tells me that I have not been conquered by despair, but lifted up in the hope of what the future holds. It tells me of the healing power of forgiveness— God's forgiveness to me, and my forgiveness to others. And it tells me that God loves me and that love is not dependent upon anything that I do.

The brown box is a reminder to me of a sad little man whom I learned to love when I learned to forgive. My rebellion hurt me far more than it hurt him—I'm sure he never missed the quarters.

The child's ring was his honest effort to please, his misplaced attempt to teach responsibility.

The wedding rings remind me that God's decisions are always the right ones. I learned many lessons about love from my life with Mike, and even more from my life with David. And the life I have lived since has been more rewarding and fulfilling than I ever knew that life could be.

The picture tells me that no matter what the circumstances, God is able to turn *everything* to good. Romans 8:28 is true. We don't see the end from the beginning, but He does. That doesn't mean that we can never suffer or question. But it can help us to take our eyes off the immediate and trust that the future will resolve itself according to His will if we will only yield ourselves to it. He will never offer us up for adoption to another. He will never give well-intentioned but less than perfect gifts, nor will he give them conditionally. And it reminds me that while God cares about all of our days, He is not nearly as concerned about the past, where we've been, as He is about the future, the directions we are heading.

Some who read these pages will have a desire to correspond with me. Please, feel free to do so. You may contact me through Zondervan with complete assurance that all correspondence will remain confidential. The address to use is:

> Katherine Edwards
> c/o Zondervan Publishing House
> Editorial Offices
> 1415 Lake Drive, S.E.
> Grand Rapids, MI 49506

NOTES

Chapter 1 *The Why of It All*

¹*Time,* 7 September 1981, 69.
²Ibid.
³Ibid.
⁴*Newsweek,* 30 November 1981, 68.

Chapter 7 *Annie's Children*

¹Mary De Young, *The Sexual Victimization of Children* (Jefferson, N.C.: McFarland and Co. Inc., 1982), 18–19.
²Ibid., 54–55.
³Ibid., 27–30.

Chapter 9 *Families That Hurt*

¹Jill Warren-Gertiser, *Community Child Abuse Prevention Plan for Kent County* (Grand Rapids: Kent County Council for the Prevention of Child Abuse and Neglect, 1987), 22.
²Ibid., 5.
³Richard E. Butman, "Hidden Victims: The Facts About Incest," *His* (April 1983): 21.
⁴Robert L. Geiser, *Hidden Victims: The Sexual Abuse of Children* (Boston: Beacon Press, 1979), 44.
⁵Gerald D. Erickson and Terrence P. Hogan, eds., *Family Therapy: An Introduction to Theory and Technique* (Belmont, Calif.: Wadworth Publishing Co., Inc., 1972), 111–12.
⁶De Young, *Sexual Victimization,* 12.
⁷Ibid.
⁸Ibid.
⁹Ibid, 10–11

[10]Henry Giaretto, *Child Sexual Abuse Treatment Program* (San Jose, Calif.: Institute for the Community as Extended Family), 3–6.

[11]De Young, *Sexual Victimization*, 16.

[12]Ellen Weber, "Incest," *Ms.* (April 1977): 7.

[13]Geiser, *Hidden Victims*, 13.

Chapter 10 *From "Dear Daddy" to "Abba Father"*

[1]Genesis 39:9b.

[2]Genesis 45:8.

[3]De Young, *Sexual Victimization*, 53.

[4]Gary Collins, *Christian Counseling: A Comprehensive Guide* (Waco, Tex.: Word, Inc., 1980), 40–41.

[5]De Young, *Sexual Victimization*, 63.

[6]Ibid.

[7]Zig Ziglar, *See You at the Top* (Gretna, La.: Pelican Pub. Co., 1981).

[8]De Young, *Sexual Victimization*, 49.

Chapter 11 *The Conclusion of It All*

[1]Unnumbered Bulletin, YWCA, Grand Rapids, Mich.

[2]Ruth S. Kempe and C. Henry Kempe, *Child Abuse* (Cambridge, Mass.: Harvard University Press, 1978), 67.

[3]4C SCAN, Grand Rapids, Mich.

[4]Amy Carmichael, *His Thoughts Said ... His Father Said* (Fort Washington, Pa.: Christian Literature Crusade), 22.

RECOMMENDED READING

Carter, W. Leslie, Paul D. Meier, and Frank B. Minirth. *Why Be Lonely? A Guide to Meaningful Relationships*. Grand Rapids: Baker Book House, 1982.

Landorf, Joyce. *Irregular People*. Waco, Texas: Word Books, 1982.

Scheflen, Albert E., M.D., with Alice Scheflen. *Body Language and Social Order: Communication as Behavioral Control*. Englewood Cliffs, New Jersey: Prentice-Hall, Inc., 1972.

Smith, Joyce Marie. *Fulfillment*. Wheaton, Illinois: Tyndale House Pub. Inc., 1975.

Towner, Jason. *Forgiveness Is for Giving*. Nashville, Tennessee: Impact Books, 1982.

Ziglar, Zig. *See You at the Top*. Gretna, Louisiana: Pelican Pub. Co., 1981.